History of Children's Costume

ELIZABETH EWING

Bibliophile, *London*

To my grandsons
Piers Harper Milligan and
Francis Quoys Milligan

First published 1977
Reprinted 1982
© Elizabeth Ewing 1977

Filmset by Servis Filmsetting Ltd, Manchester
Printed in Great Britain by
The Anchor Press Ltd, Tiptree, Essex
Published by Bibliophile,
33 Maiden Lane, London WC2E 7JS
by arrangement with
B. T. Batsford Ltd, London

Contents

List of Illustrations

List of colour plates

Acknowledgments

The author and publishers wish to thank the following for permission to reproduce the illustrations included in this book: Babygro for 113 and 114; Lord Bearsted and the National Trust for 26; Birmingham Museum and Art Gallery for 35; British Home Stores for 110 and 111; Sir George Burns for 15; Chilprufe for 91, 94 and 108; Christ's Hospital Girls' School for 17; Courtauld Institute of Art and the National Trust, Hardwick Hall for 11; Lord De L'Isle for 14 and colour plate 1; Glencoe and North Lorn Folk Museum for 85; Lena Harper for 50, 56, 59, 64; Frances Jackson for 60; Ladybird for 109; London College of Fashion Library for 70, 101, 112 and 119; Mansell Collection for 13, 37, 43, 52, 63, 72, 86 and 90; Mothercare for 115 and 116; Museum of Costume, Bath for 25, 45, 51, 69, 71, 92, 93, 95, 96, 106, 107 and colour plate 4; National Monuments Record (Crown Copyright) for 4 and 5; National Film Archive for 99 and 103; National Portrait Gallery for 18 and 19; North London Collegiate School for 102; Popperfoto for 16, 87, 98, 104, 105, 120, 121 and 122; H.M. The Queen for 58; Ronald Searle for 2; Earl Spencer for 28; Tate Gallery for 21, 32 and colour plates 2 and 3; Anne Tritton for 80; Victoria and Albert Museum for 9, 10, 22, 23, 24, 31, 33, 36, 38, 39, 40, 42, 44, 46, 49, 53, 54, 55, 73, 74, 78 and 88; Viyella for 117 and 118; Lord Willoughby de Broke for 29.

The remaining illustrations have been taken from the collections of the author and the publishers.

Preface

In the title and text of this book the word children is used reluctantly, in-accurately and unsatisfactorily to describe all non-adults. The inadequate and unpopular word has been adopted because no other term gives an umbrella description of all ages below adulthood. The further complication that the word adult admits of different definitions in law and in past and present usage is unfortunately insoluble.

A word with all-over coverage was required by a book which aims not only at describing the kind of clothes worn through the centuries by young people from infancy until they were grown-up but also at enquiring into the many factors, historical, social, psychological and technical, which have influenced and even conditioned the clothes of various age groups of the young at different periods.

Throughout history, until the last twenty or thirty years, children, unlike adults, had no real say in what they wore. Their fashions and general attire reflected adult attitudes to childhood and not, except by indoctrination, the attitudes of children themselves. In this important respect the story of children's costume differs from the rest of costume history. In its evolution a variety of age groups have moved towards a liberation of their dress at different times, for different reasons and at different rates. Therefore a comprehensive word had to be found and it had to be children.

It has never been a popular word. In the seventeenth century, Alice Meynell has pointed out, 'Evelyn and his contemporaries dropped the very word child as soon as might be, if not sooner. When a poor little boy came to be eight years old they called him a youth.' Nearly 300 years later, in 1947, the trade publication launched in 1936 as *The Children's Outfitter* changed its name to *Junior Age* because its name still had a wrong connotation.

To start with, therefore, apologies are tendered to all infants, poppets and moppets, youngsters, kids, juniors, boys and girls, lads and lassies, teeny-boppers, bobbysoxers, sub-teenagers and teenagers who are described as children and who could very reasonably object to being grouped together under a term not only largely outdated and often inapplicable to them but also, by its associations, disparaging to them as people forming part of the community and entitled to have a say in what they wear and in their other activities from their earliest articulate years.

Next, for help and guidance in developing the theme of this book I have been deeply indebted to many people for information, personal recollections and family photographs. Specifically I should like to record my appreciation of the assistance given to me by the staffs of the Bethnal Green Museum of Childhood and the Fawcett Library; Mr Lawrence Jones of the Historic Churches Preservation Trust; Mrs Muriel Ross and the staff of the London College of Fashion Library; Mrs M. Legrand and Mrs Myra Mines of the Museum of Costume, Bath and Miss Penelope Byrde of the Research Centre there; the staffs of Ruislip Library, Uxbridge Library and the Victoria and Albert Museum Library and Department of Textiles. To Dr Rosalind E. Marshall and Collins I am grateful for permission to quote from *The Days of the Duchess Anne.*

I also owe a debt of gratitude to Mr Michael Stephenson of B.T. Batsford for his constant interest and his sound judgment on numerous points of interpretation of costume, and finally, to Mrs Kathleen Bawden who from considerable disarray produced an excellent typescript of this history.

1 Swaddling and Subjugation

When, in 1975, Ronald Searle spoke on television about the most famous schoolgirls of all time and the most successful of all his cartoon creations, the girls of St Trinians of 20 to 30 years ago, he suggested that they owed their immense popularity to the fact that 'it was, perhaps, the first time in the history of cartooning that someone had simply stated that children could be cruel, disgusting, revolting, inconceivably un-nineteenth-century childlike'. As a cartoonist he was probably right, but as a description of children his was only the latest return to the view held very widely through history and prevalent in Britain until about 150 years ago. Children not only could be all these things, they were usually assumed to be so. Children were full of original sin which had to be driven out of them by the utmost rigour and severity. Childhood was a regrettable prelude to maturity, to be got over as quickly as possible. To achieve this, young people were encouraged to behave and look like miniature adults. If they belonged to the upper classes, education and discipline were drilled into them from the nursery stage. If poor, they

1 Early children's dress was a smaller version of that of adults. From a medieval manuscript

2   The Girls of St Trinians, the most famous of all schoolgirls, created by Ronald Searle in a Japanese prisoner-of-war camp in 1941

were put to work equally prematurely. And at the earliest possible age they were dressed almost identically as adults in the fashions of the time.

From the present vantage point more than three quarters through what has so often been called the century of the child it is generally taken for granted that the clothes of the young should be their own kind of clothes, designed for their own way of life, comfortable, healthy, easy-care and, as soon as the child is capable of expressing an opinion, partly if not wholly chosen, or at least approved of, by the wearer. This has even extended recently to school uniforms, which used to be prescribed by the powers that be.

This is, however, an innovation, part of a general new recognition of the child as an individual, a distinct entity with his own rights and needs, which should be met. Such recognition emerged late and slowly, and the long lack of it was reflected in the way children's clothes for centuries tagged along in the pageant of costume as a mere smaller version of those of their elders. The child had no say in what he wore, as adults had, so his clothes had no real history of their own and only in a negative way recorded a childhood story. As recently as 1952 anthropologist Margaret Mead in *The Contemporary American Family* found it new and worthy of note that 'Within the family children are given an extraordinary amount of attention, when judged by the standards of most other societies. Their needs, their wishes and their performances are regarded as central and worthy of adult attention.'

The emancipation of the child has been part of an immense social revolution which began about 200 years ago and is still going on, and the development of his particular kind of dressing from that time onwards has been an outward and visible sign of his changed status. In the long and complicated attainment of this victory the child has even to some degree been the father of the man, leading the way to the general adoption of comfortable clothes for the first time in the fashion history of our era. Those girls of St Trinians were, of course, as beastly as any old-time children ever were thought to be, but the point is that they were a joke. There was none of the erstwhile moral opprobrium about them, no grim zeal for reform. They were cartoon stuff and no more.

The history of children's clothes is a worthwhile human study only in so far as it contributes to a better understanding of children. Early material for such a study is often sparse. Even in Tudor times, when general social progress was considerable, very little is on record about children and their lives. 'The child's infant progress was deemed of too little interest or importance to his family to merit record. Hence we know very little about the sort of lives very young children led', say Ivy Pinchbeck and Margaret Hewitt in their *Children In English Society*. The enormous infant mortality, which persisted until last century, and the general brevity of life (on average, 30 years), both of which helped to force children into the adult world at the age of between seven and nine, were, they point out, among the main reasons for the lack of knowledge about early children. The low status of women and the lack of birth control also made it difficult for the best-intentioned to achieve happy, understanding parenthood. Many, however, did, and left records of it.

That such records, at least through earlier history, relate mainly to the upper classes, is almost inevitable in these conditions. A contented, loved

3 Nothing youthful about these children, dressed like their elders. From a medieval manuscript

4   Swaddling was practised for centuries. The monument at Stoke D'Abernon church, Surrey, to Ellen Bray, a Christian child, 1576

and satisfied childhood was, and, to some degree still remains, a luxury enjoyed only by a few in the world as a whole. Much of the history of the rest, how they lived and how they looked, is largely untold or fragmentary. It was never the century of the child. Writers on costume have continually deplored the scarcity of information on the clothes of past children. Typical is the well-informed and thoughtful Mrs Merrifield who, writing in 1854, said: 'While the history of male and female costume of adults, both in England and the continent, has been amply investigated and illustrated, that of children remains in obscurity, either from a scarcity of materials, or a want of interest in the subject itself. Portraits of children are rare, compared with those of adults; the few which we can recall to our recollection are like small editions of the portraits of men and women; they have nothing youthful about them but their faces, and even these are grave and formal, as the gravity of their habiliments seems to require. They are little old men and women, in spite of their youthful faces. It is not until we come to the pictures of Sir Joshua Reynolds that we really find representations of children, and, in fact, it is not always the case in his.'

There was, however, one vital and continuous exception to the identification of the dress of the child with that of the adult. Until well into the eighteenth century, by which time western adult fashion had been cavorting in innumerable guises for more than 300 years, infants were still spending the first part of their existence in the swaddling bands of biblical times and probably of innumerable centuries before this in most parts of the world. These bands, which varied very little through history, and which turned the child into a tight cocoon, unable to move in any direction, were used with a tenacity which resisted generations of reformers. They had the considerable convenience of allowing the mother or nurse to carry the little parcel around with some degree of safety, to deposit it at will and, if need be, to hang it up on a peg, as was in fact done. There was also a grossly mistaken but probably often honest belief that tight binding would not only protect the child from falls and other accidents but would also encourage the straightness of legs and arms, which were at times all encompassed in the bands. That the child might suffer perilously from lack of freedom and exercise and even die in the convulsions of frustration, pain or fury seems not to have been considered.

The child's costume story therefore starts with a complete denial of physical freedom, a total subjection, and with a practice which inhibited healthy growth and had nothing whatever in its favour from the child's point of view.

Swaddling was generally adopted by all classes of society, though, as in all early history, surviving records show it mainly among the high-born because the annals of the poor were not so much short and simple as simply non-existent. A ninth-century manuscript, reproduced by Joseph Strutt in his *A Complete View of the Dress and Habits of the People of England*, depicts a coroneted lady handing a tightly trussed-up baby to a girl, evidently a nursemaid. Many similar pictures survive in early manuscripts, which are a main source of information on the subject. A picture by Matthew Prior of Edmund, son of Henry III, shows a child swaddled and lying in an elaborate fourposter-style cot. Church effigies and memorials throughout Britain record similar examples of the practice of swaddling. A Chinese pottery figure of AD 1280 shows an Eastern baby similarly encased.

A description of the process is quoted by Rosamond Bayne-Powell in *The English Child in the Eighteenth Century*. It tells how 'a strong cotton swathe about six inches in width and ten to twelve feet long was . . . wound tightly round the baby's body beginning at the armpits and going down to the hips. This, it was thought, would keep its spine straight, and prevent the infant from breaking its legs, as it assuredly would do, if it were allowed to kick them about. The tighter the swaddling clothes were pulled the better it was for the child, and in some cases the arms were enclosed as well.'

The history of swaddling is surveyed in detail in *A History of Domestic Manners and Sentiments in England during the Middle Ages*, published in 1862 and written by Dr Thomas Wright, a considerable authority and member of many learned societies. For early Anglo-Saxon times he can find few records of swaddling, but concludes that 'probably it differed little from the general practice of a later period'. He adds that 'the pernicious practice of swathing or swaddling the child as soon as it was born prevailed everywhere, and the infant was kept in this condition until it became necessary to teach it the use of its limbs.' He quotes a late thirteenth-century Anglo-Norman

5 A memorial church brass of 1605 at Wormington, Glos. shows mother and swaddled baby

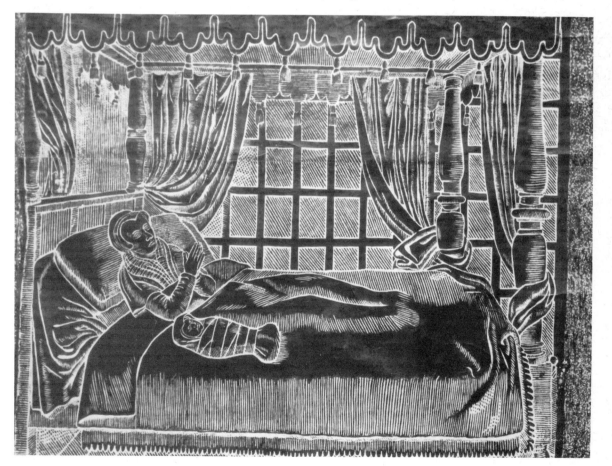

OCTOBRIS 1634 · ÆTATIS SVÆ 29°

6 Swaddling combined with the wearing of clothes is seen in this church monument of 1634 in the church of Earl's Combe, Worcestershire

author Walter de Bibblesworth who, writing in French, as was often done at the time, stated: 'As soon as the child is born it must be swathed; lay it to sleep in its cradle, and you must have a nurse to rock it to sleep.' Dr Wright continues: 'This was the manner in which the new-born infant was treated in all grades of society.' Summing up, he concludes: 'The custom of swatheling children in their infancy, though evidently injurious as well as ridiculous, has prevailed from a very early period, and is still practised in some parts of Europe.' He gives the derivation of the word 'swathel' as the Anglo-Saxon 'beswethan', to swathe or bind, and explains 'swethel' or 'swaethel' as a swaddling band. He finds a reference to the binding of the infant Christ 'with cloths wound round' in the Exeter Book and a picture of a child being prepared to be swaddled by its mother in the Anglo-Saxon manuscript of Caedmon, the first English poet on record, who died in 680. A clear picture of a child tightly swaddled in criss-cross bands is also illustrated from a fourteenth-century manuscript.

To what age swaddling was continued is not, Mr Wright says, on record, but Walter de Bibblesworth states that a child is left free to crawl before it can walk:

Le enfant covent de chatouner
Avaunt de fache à pées-aler.

The needs of nature must have called for frequent unwrapping of the human parcel even when hygiene was crude, and swaddling was at times relaxed to allow the child to enjoy his natural instinct for healthy kicking. It could also be combined with something like a layette. Among dialogues written by Claudius Hollyband and Peter Erondell, two Huguenot refugees who taught French in London in the 1560s, a charming and affectionate nursery item of 1568 by Erondell includes a passage in which a mother, addressing the nurse, says: 'How now, how doeth the childe? . . . Unswathe him, undoe his swadling bands, . . . wash him before me. Pull off his shirt, . . . Now swadle him againe, but first put on his biggin [a head covering, like a coif], and his little band [collar] with an edge, where is his little petticote? Give him his coate of changeable [shot] taffeta and his satin sleeves: where is his bibbe? Let him have his gathered aprone with stringes, and hang a muckinder [handkerchief] to it. You need not yet to give him his corall with the small gold chayne, for I believe it is better to let him sleepe untill the afternoone . . . God send thee sound rest my little boykin.' Coral, incidentally, was from the remote past to modern times used for children's rattles and beads, and was believed to bring luck.

A considerable number of other garments especially devised for infants can be recorded from Tudor times. This was in line with the growing sophistication of clothes and in particular with the ardent Tudor cultivation of the art of needlework and embroidery among ladies of the period. A sixteenth-century midwife is on record as asking for 'swaddling bands' in a large list of infants' garments. How complicated swaddling could be is recorded by Barbara Aeton who, in a *Bulletin of the Costume Society of Scotland*, detailed the process from instructions given by Lady Nithsdale, who had charge of the young family of James III, the Old Pretender, during his exile in Rome in the first quarter of the eighteenth century. For an anticipated birth she ordered items for five main processes involved in swaddling. First a shirt, open in front: then a 'bed', which was a square band, bound round the baby's breast down to its feet and up again; next a roller, which was a long swaddling band; a tube-like waistcoat which pinioned the arms; a second roller and finally a blanket. This seems to explain the elaborate parcel-like wrappings seen in some effigies and paintings of babies, which often bear no resemblance to the visible swaddled look.

Quite a considerable variety of actual baby clothes are in existence from the seventeenth century and are preserved in various museums. The Victoria and Albert Museum has some of the earliest of all, those which belonged to the infancy of Charles II. In the finest cambric, exquisitely sewn with near-invisible stitches, they also have hem-stitching and feather-stitching and are complete down to tiny lace mittens. The same museum has a seventeenth-century child's vest in fine knitted wool, almost like a matinee coat of today, and, like many other little vests and shirts of the time, sensibly opening down the front. There are also little lawn caps and small squares and triangles worn on the head and described as 'forehead cloths'. Covering the head was regarded as very important then and for long afterwards. A set of seventeenth-century clothes includes forehead cloths, robe, chemise, shirts, collars, caps, bibs and separate dickey-style fronts for dresses. As white and fresh as when they were made, they were worn by the children of Sir Thomas Remington of Lund, Yorkshire, who was born in 1611 and by 1647 had a large family.

The Gallery of Costume at Platt Hall, Manchester, has examples of babywear dating from the seventeenth century, most of it small items like caps, bibs and mittens, which are the main survivals. The Museum of Costume at Bath, with two tiny shirts, mittens and bibs of the sixteenth century, probably has the earliest extant examples of what infants wore. It also has beautifully embroidered and lace-trimmed baby accessories of the seventeenth century, including the small triangular forehead pieces worn under caps. From the eighteenth century it has silk caps embroidered in coloured thread, bonnets, little coats and an Empire-style robe.

Britain was evidently a pioneer in limiting the period of swaddling, though it was not actually dropped for a long time to come. Evidence for this comes in a statement on the care of children made by Madame de Maintenon, who was responsible for the upbringing of several of Louis XIV's illegitimate children. At the age of 72, in 1707, she wrote in a letter: 'If I were not so old I would have liked to try bringing up children as they do in England, where they are all tall and well built, and as we have seen them brought up at St Germain.' This was a reference to the exiled Court of King James II of England, which she knew. She goes on to explain what she means about English children: 'When they are two or three months old they are no longer tightly swaddled, but under their dress they wear a wrapper and a loose nappy, which are changed as soon as they are soiled, so that the infants never remain, as ours do, tightly swaddled in their own mess. In consequence they never cry, are upset, suffer from sores or even have their little limbs deformed.' An optimistic picture, but it includes an important statement of fact.

Condemnation of swaddling on health grounds became widespread after this, both among those who spoke with authority and among humbler folk. One of the most prominent attackers of the practice was John Locke, in his *Thoughts Concerning Education* (1693). This achieved wide attention and the extent of its circulation is shown by the fact that even Pamela, the heroine of Richardson's famous novel, who was a servant girl and no intellectual, had heard of it and strongly supported Locke's views on the unhealthiness of swaddling infants. 'How has my heart ached many and many a time when I have seen poor babies rolled and swathed, ten or a dozen times round; then blanket upon blanket, mantle upon that; its little neck pinned down to one position, . . . its legs and arms . . . the former bundled upon, the latter pinned down; and how the poor thing lies on the nurse's lap, a miserable little pinioned captive.'

The custom, however, died hard. In a typical family record of educated upper class life of the time, *The Parkers at Saltram (1769–1789)*, Theresa Parker, awaiting her second confinement, accepted, though reluctantly, the fact that the traditional régime would have to be followed when her child was born. 'A child,' she said in a letter, 'is no sooner born than it is bound up as firmly as an Egyptian mummy in folds of linen . . . in vain for him to give signs of distress . . . the old witch who presides over his infant days winds him up in his destined confinement.'

Rousseau's *Emile* (1762), which was translated into English in two simultaneous versions in the following year, had a huge influence on children's upbringing and on their clothing, as will be shown later. It started with a detailed description of swaddling and an outright condemnation which, although it echoed what had already often been said, was expressed with great force and attracted more attention than had any of his predecessors. 'The child,' he says, 'has hardly left the mother's womb, it has hardly begun to move and stretch its limbs, when it is deprived of its freedom. It is wrapped in swaddling bands, laid down with its head fixed, its legs stretched out, and its arms by its side; it is wound round with linen and bandages of all sorts so that it cannot move.' Against this all his passions are roused: swaddling leads to ailments and deformities, it kills children, it is adopted to make life easy for lazy nurses. However, he writes of France and adds in a footnote that in England 'the senseless and barbarous swaddling clothes have become almost obsolete'. Not quite though, even then. As late as 1813 a minor poet, the Rev. Weedon Butler, Jnr, wrote some verses on the birth of his fifth child, putting the words into the mouth of the baby concerned, who laments leaving the womb where

> *'Tis true I could not stretch my hands and feet*
> *But ah! nor nurse nor swaddling-bands annoyed.*

In the same poem the child goes on to lament being

> *enslav'd to female power,*
> *Lapp'd, fondled, sooth'd, kiss'd, patted and carest,*
> *Then – all within the compass of an hour –*
> *Pinion'd and truss'd, swath'd, manacled and drest.*

There are references to swaddling as at least a remembered practice in a number of Victorian books on costume and child welfare, and to this day the custom persists to some degree in peasant communities in various parts of the world, including Eastern Europe. At Patras, in Greece, a few years ago, a surprised tourist's visit to the church there coincided with the baptism, by full-scale immersion, of a screaming infant, previously laid on the ground and elaborately unwound from the tight ages-old cocoon of his swaddling clothes for the ceremony. In *My Family and other Animals* Gerald Durrell noted, in a vast crowd assembled in honour of Corfu's patron saint, St Spiridion, 'babies wrapped and bound like cocoons'. That too was well within the present century. The swaddled baby therefore takes his unquestioned place as the first figure in the children's costume story, and probably the last to be liberated from the discomforts which have attended so much of that story until recent times.

2 Copying Adult Fashions

Recorded and surviving clothing of early children relates, to the sorrow of the social historian, mainly to royalty and the nobility. Thus the baby King Henry VI is seen in an old painting at the age of seven months held in the arms of his guardian, in a long dress, but with a crown on his little bald head. A description of fifteenth-century Royal christening robes, quoted by Herbert Norris, specifies 'a velvet cloak . . . which must be at least three ells long and must be furred with miniver . . . there must be put over the child (when the person carrying it has it on her arm) a long converchef or kerchief of violet silk extending from the child's head down to the ground.'

Ordinary children probably fared better, as far as comfort went, than noble ones, in being allowed more freedom in life and dress. Tacitus, writing of the Saxons, *c.* 100 AD, says: 'In every house you may see little boys, sons of lords

7 Happy children seen at play in a fourteenth-century manuscript

or peasants, equally ill-clad, lying about or playing among the cattle.' It is comforting to know that even the high-born could sometimes be allowed to be natural and run wild. A number of pictures in early manuscripts show chubby little boys playing games and running about in simple short tunics; a few more depict boys in longer tunics and occasionally girls too dressed somewhat similarly. Strutt shows a small thirteenth-century boy dressed for winter in a dark coat with long sleeves and hood, oddly like today's duffle coat. Another child is seen in a pinafore, while another wears a long Inverness-style cape and a round fur hat. In warm weather loose breeches with cross-over shoulder straps, worn over a vest, seem to have been the humble small boy's usual attire. They provide a close prototype for the jeans and T-shirts which have become almost a uniform for the youth of the later twentieth century.

8   Comfortable tunic worn by child for a game in an early drawing

These tunics, of varying lengths, and the coats and cloaks seen with them are, however, not distinctively children's clothes, but simply early illustrations of the fact that for centuries there were no such clothes. Adults up to the fourteenth century were wearing similar attire, and country people and some children continued to dress in that manner long after many adults had adopted quite different styles. These styles, which we commonly call fashion, began to emerge in the fourteenth century. Until then western people of both sexes and all ages wore clothes which were basically long lengths of material, tunic-style or cloak-style, with little shaping except holes for arms and head and sometimes loose straight sleeves and girdles or belts at the waist. Basic underwear was a similar tunic, though boys and men from Saxon times often also wore braies, loose trousers which were worn under the tunic and ranked

9   Little difference between the
attire of children and adults in
Tudor times

as underwear. For the majority of people, clothes were made of various types of hand-spun wool or linen; for the rich pride of place went to silk, satin and velvet, mostly imported from Italy, France and, as time went on, from the East. Men, boys and girls usually had short hair, reaching to the neck, but older girls by the fifteenth century began to follow their mothers with long hair. Shoes were flat, usually pumps or moccasins in style, with no heels until the 1580s.

As women's dress became shaped to the waist in the fourteenth century, so did girls'. This shaping was the start of the cycle of fashion in the present era. As men's dress from this time also became more elaborate and developed a complex and spectacular history, boys likewise followed their fathers. For this reason, which in itself is evidence of the limited amount of attention given to children's needs, records of early children's clothes are sparse and tend simply to blue-print what is said of adults. 'In the second half of the fourteenth century new styles evolved and boys of the upper classes, having grown out of infancy, were dressed like their fathers', say Phillis Cunnington and Anne Buck in their detailed study of youthful clothes of past times. They point out that records of what girls wore are even more scarce than those of boys, but 'in the fifteenth century girls, as far as is known, were dressed like their mothers, with some modifications'. These meant mainly a slight relaxation towards ease and simpler head coverings than the complicated ones women rejoiced in.

The elaborate and fantastically rich adult fashions of Tudor and Elizabethan times were followed closely by the children of the high-born and of the wealthy rising merchant classes, who had a monopoly of fashion. What this meant, at least in the number of garments involved, is shown by a description of the requirements of the young Princess Elizabeth. On the execution of her mother, Anne Boleyn, the three-year-old future Queen had been entrusted to the care of Lady Bryan and was soon evidently being neglected by her father, Henry VIII. A letter written by Lady Bryan to Thomas Cromwell soon after she had taken charge of the child and found among the State papers of the period pleads for the needs of the child, 'beseeching . . . that she may have some raiment. For she hath neither gown, nor kirtle, nor peticoat, nor no maner of linen, nor fore-smocks [pinafores], nor kerchefs, nor rails [night-gowns], nor body stitchets [corsets], nor handkerchiefs, nor sleeves, nor mufflers [mob caps], nor biggens [night caps].' A complicated wardrobe for a three or four year old!

Although he was, by the standards of the time, a near-adult when he died at 17, Henry Fitzroy, Duke of Richmond and Somerset, Henry VIII's son by Elizabeth Blount, left a wardrobe which illustrates the richness and complexity of youthful attire at that time. It contained four gowns, nine coats, six doublets, eight pairs of hose and numerous hats, bonnets, boots, swords and daggers. One gown was of purple velvet, lined with yellow silk and embroidered in gold, and there was also a 'hole furre of sables' and a 'hole furre of pampillion and black Bogye'.

The child as a miniature adult, the image that was to last until the latter part of the eighteenth century, had arrived. From now onwards there are increasing records of how he or she looked. Church effigies become more numerous, as do family portraits, mostly groups in which, rather surprisingly,

10 Mother and daughters dressed almost identically in a 1550 church brass at Clapham, Essex

11   In 1577 two-year-old Lady
Arbella Stuart, daughter of the
Earl of Lennox, follows fashion,
as does her doll

the unchildlike children often have a central position. But valuable as these are, they do not tell the full story of actual children's clothes, and are probably even misleading, because they show children of high rank, dressed in their best for a special occasion. For most of the population life was rural and probably everyday clothes for children of all classes came close to a simple, timeless peasant dress. There is some evidence that girls of rank would doff their silks and satins and go about their play in the holland shifts worn by girls of humble origin, while high-born boys seem to have worn the peasant-style smocks and braies of peasant children. Echoes of this occur in the way children's clothes developed when they took off in their own direction in the eighteenth century.

Meantime, however, certain features emerged to distinguish the clothes of children and to meet their special needs. One was, the 'pudding', also called the 'black pudding'. It was a common item of wear for children for a long period, at least up to the eighteenth century. A detailed description of it is given by that rambling but spicy gossip, J.T. Smith, in his reminiscences, *Book for a Rainy Day*, first published in 1845, 12 years after his death. A further note about it occurs in *Nollekens and his Times*, his biography of the sculptor, Joseph Nollekens. The full description states that in 1768 'at the age when most children place things on their heads and say "Hot pies", I displayed a black pudding upon mine, which my mother, careful soul, had provided for its protection in case I should fall. This is another article mentioned in *Nollekens and his Times*; and having there stated that Rubens, in a picture at Blenheim, had painted one on the head of a son of his . . . and as the mothers of future days may wish to know its shape, I beg to inform them that there is an engraving of it by MacArdell. But . . . it would be . . . difficult to produce a similar black pudding to mine, were I not to state that it was made of a long narrow piece of black silk or satin, padded with wadding, and then formed to

12   Sixteenth-century boys dressed simply for everyday games

13   The 'pudding' or 'black
pudding' as shown by Rubens,
c.1620. The MacArdell engraving

the head according to the taste of the parent, or similar to that of little Rubens.'
A footnote adds that Nollekens said 'I wore a pudding when I was a little boy,
and all my mother's children wore puddings'.

Reins, still used to some extent today to prevent little feet from straying
into peril, have a long history. A crimson pair made by Mary Queen of Scots
for the little James VI, whom she never saw after the age of a year and whose
first faltering steps she therefore never had the chance to guide, survive among
Stuart relics and have been exhibited during this century.

Hanging sleeves, long and empty, in front of which the arms appeared in
separate, simpler sleeves, are an odd feature of Elizabethan and later children's
dress based on adult styles. Such sleeves came to be referred to as a symbol of
childishness, the phrase 'in hanging sleeves' being used by Pepys to describe
young girls, and also of second childhood. They may have been an endeavour
to bring a little ease into the uncomfortable adult fashions worn by children,
but they were also used as reins, and are seen in this guise in some paintings.

Another distinctive childish item seen in many pictures was the muckinder,
already mentioned by Erondell in 1568. It was a large man-size handkerchief
usually attached to the waist of the dress by one corner and hanging down to
the floor-length hem. It must have had many uses, and it survived to be seen
in eighteenth-century paintings as well as in earlier drawings and effigies,
Aprons are also often seen in children's portraits, even of the formal kind, but
women also sometimes wore them.

The biggest distinction between the child and the adult was, however, one
that occurred inside the shared fashion scene. It was that, until well into the
eighteenth century, boys were dressed almost exactly like girls in their early
years, sometimes until the age of about six. Family portraits galore show such
boys in the same full-length bell-shaped skirts as their sisters and mothers,
though they do not seem to have worn either the Elizabethan farthingale,

14   Farthingales for the two
older girls, a long sword for the
boy still in petticoats, and
simpler fashions for the smaller
members of the family of Sir
Robert Sidney, later Earl of
Leicester (1563–1626), with their
mother, about 1600

15   Boys and girls dressed alike in this portrait of three children of James VI and I: Henry, Charles and Elizabeth (later Elizabeth of Bohemia), aged five, two and four respectively. Inscribed 1611, it shows the elder boy carrying a tiny sword at his hip, while the younger has a doll

sometimes seen on small girls, or the eighteenth-century panniers, likewise shown on girls. Sometimes the boys' bodices were similar to those of the girls, at others they had a hint of manliness in doubtlet-style designs borrowed from their fathers. A tiny sword is sometimes girt across the dress with its girlish skirt. Underneath would be the chemise common to both sexes for centuries, as was the corset, even for the youngest, for formal wear. These small boys in ankle-length dresses appear in paintings for three centuries, invariably and with not a single exception.

Sir Richard Steele, the essayist and dramatist (1672–1729), wrote to his wife about his son, who could already read his *Primer* and was interested in the pictures in Virgil: 'I hope I shall be pardoned if I equip him with new cloathes and frocks.' This may, however, have meant the wide-skirted coat of the time, perpetuated in the 'frock coat', though 'frock' was until well into the nineteenth century used for children's, but not adults' dresses.

To dress small boys like girls seems to contradict the fact that every effort was made to turn the child into an adult as soon as possible. But until the age of about six the child was usually in the care of women, and this is probably the reason for his being in skirts or petticoats – from which came the common description of the boy still being 'in coats', which did not mean coats at all in the modern sense.

The process of 'breeching' at the age of about six, when the boy shed his petticoats, was a proud family occasion, recorded in detail in many memoirs of the seventeenth century and later. In *A Winter's Tale*, too, Leontes, speaking of his little son, Mamilius, a very articulate small boy, says:

> *Looking on the lines*
> *Of my boy's face, methought I did recoil*
> *Twenty-three years, and saw myself unbreeched,*
> *In my green velvet coat, my dagger muzzled*
> *Lest it should bite its master, and so prove,*
> *As ornaments oft do, too dangerous.*
> *How like, methought, I then was to this kernel,*
> *This squash, this gentleman.*

The coat, again, means a petticoat or skirt.

Sir Henry Slingsby wrote in his diary in 1641: 'I sent from London against Easter a suite of cloaths for my son Thomas, being ye first breeches and doublet yt he ever had, and made by my tailor, Mr. Miller, it was too soon for him to wear ym being but 5 years old but yt his mother had a desire to see him in ym how proper a man he would be.' There is also a particularly delightful description of a breeching given in a letter sent to Lord Chief Justice Sir Francis North, later Lord Guilford, Lord Keeper of the Great Seal of England, on 10 October 1679 by a loving grandmother, Anne, Lady North. Her account of the 'leaving off of coats' by his motherless six-year-old son, Francis, called 'little Frank', had been preceded in March 1678 by a letter saying 'Frank will have his breeches ere long'. After the great day she wrote: 'You cannot beleeve the great concerne that was in the whole family here last Wednesday, it being the day that the Taylor was to helpe to dress little Frank in his breeches in order to the making an everyday suit by it. Never had any bride that was to be drest upon her wedding night more hands about her, some the legs, some the armes, the taylore butt'ning and other putting on the sword, and so many lookers on that had I not had a ffinger amongst them I could not have seen him. When he was quite drest he looked his part as well as any of them, for he desired he might goe downe to inquire for the little gentleman that was here the day before in a black coat, and speak to the men to tell the gentleman when he came from school that here was a gallant with very fine cloths and a sword to have waited upon him and would come upon Sunday next . . . They are very fit, everything, and he looks taler and prettyer than in his coats. Little Charles rejoyced as much as he did, for he jumpt all the while about him and took notice of everything. I went to Bury and bo't everything for another suit, which will be finisht upon Saturday so that coats are to be quite left off upon Sunday.' There is a final point: 'When he was drest he asked Buckle whether muffs were out of fashion because they had not sent him one'; men carried muffs then. Another letter from Lady North to her son, dated 12 October, sums up the same event: 'This day was designed wholly to throw off the coats and write man.'

Once breeched, this boy went out into the world of school. In July 1688 his grandmother wrote, again to the absent father: 'I prayse God these here are very well, but grown so wild I know not how to order them, and did not Frank goe every day to school this little house would be too little for him.' A sentiment found among even the most devoted of grandmothers.

Breeching continued to be a matter for celebration for a long time. A poem, *Going into Breeches*, by Mrs Leicester, probably a pen name of Charles Lamb, says:

> *Joy to Philip, he this day*
> *Has his long coats cast away,*
> *And (the childish season gone)*
> *Put the manly breeches on.*
>
> *Sashes, frocks, to those who need 'em –*
> *Philip's limbs have got their freedom.*

The dominant theme of all the accounts of breeching is invariable; the small boy has become a 'man'. His clothes henceforth are small versions of men's clothes, following men's fashions. Girls followed women in the same way, but they simply continued in the course set from near-infancy and for them there was no comparable symbol of enfranchisement.

While the sprigs of the noble and wealthy were decked out in small-scale versions of the extravagant adult fashions of the day, what were to become the first distinctive children's clothes emerged from the unregarded and largely unrecorded area of humble life. They were the uniforms adopted by certain institutions.

The Reformation, by suppressing the monasteries, dealt a heavy blow to education, in which monastic, charity and guild schools, church-sponsored, had been prominent, especially in teaching poorer children. To counter this blow, various charitable people and reformers began to set up institutions to provide education for at least some of the deprived and in many cases distinctive outfits were provided for the pupils. The general principle underlying such uniforms was that they should, as Bishop Butler said, remind the wearers of their servile state 'and that they were the objects of charity.' These clothes, the earliest of which date from the sixteenth century, were based on styles worn by ordinary children at the time of their introduction and some of them were worn, almost unchanged, for centuries, illustrating the recurrent point that uniforms of all kinds are often frozen fashion.

The Blue Coat schools are unique in preserving the ordinary Tudor child's attire for posterity. 'Our only representative of the appearance of little boys

16 Tudor dress still worn today by boys at King's School, Canterbury

up to the sixteenth century is found in one or two educational establishments, such as the Blue Coat Schools in London', said Dr Wright in 1862. 'To this day', he continued, 'this first of all school uniforms survives almost unchanged.' Stow, in his *Survey of London* (1633) recorded in more detail that when Christ's Hospital, the original Blue Coat school and the earliest surviving charitable institution of the kind, was founded in 1552, 'in the month of November the children were taken into the same to the number of almost 400 . . . all in one livery of russett cotton . . . and at Easter next they were in blue . . . and so have continued ever since'.

Oddly it was not until 1939 that this group of uniforms was studied closely when the Rev. Wallace Clare set himself 'to place on record for the first time annotated representations of a number of the many uniforms worn by English schoolboys at various periods since the sixteenth century'. He pointed out that some still survived, 'such as the picturesque and dignified Tudor kit of the boys of Christ's Hospital (a style adopted by many English schools in the past)'. Today, 38 years further on, the uniform is still worn. It consists of a long blue coat reaching to the ankles, with a leather girdle, yellow stockings (introduced in 1638) and linen neckbands, substituted for the original Tudor ruff. It was, says Dr Clare, 'simply a survival of the ordinary attire of the children of the people and apprentices in Tudor days, and a fashion originally

17   The original uniform of the
girls of Christ's Hospital

based on the ecclesiastical cassock'. More accurately, that cassock was itself
a survival of the medieval tunic generally worn by men and boys, so the
genealogy should be reversed. From 1636 a 'kersey' or petticoat, dyed yellow,
was worn under the long tunic of Christ's Hospital boys and it survived in use
until 1837. Up to 1736 no breeches were worn under the gown, but in that
year leather ones were introduced for 'sick and weakly children' and after a
few years were universally adopted. In 1760 a rule laid down that the boys
should have 'each yearly two pairs of breeches made of Russia drab instead of
the leather breeches they now have'. A small round red or blue hat was worn
until 1857, since when heads have been bare.

Blue Coat girls, part of the original foundation, also wore for centuries a
dress based on that of Tudor girls. Like the boys, they wore at the outset
russet clothing – a uniform of 'russet cotton with kerchiefs on their heads',
but by Easter Day 1553 they had assumed the garb worn until 1875 – 'blue dress,
white, green or blue apron, white coifs and peaked caps'. Yellow stockings
were usually worn, but they varied. Since 1875 there has been continual
updating and today's pupils at what has become a very progressive and
splendidly equipped girls' school at Hertford wear a smart fashion-styled
uniform which is completely contemporary. But from niches on the walls
of their school there still look down two statues, shining with bright paint,
showing girls in the original Tudor dress. The school museum has records of
the dress at every stage, with dolls correctly dressed, detailed drawings and
actual replicas of the original outfit – the ordinary Tudor girl whom the
history books and costume historians forgot.

Many other similar early school uniforms are recorded in statues and
effigies. The Museum of London has, for instance, 'the quaint figures which
were removed from the old Faringdon Ward School. Maidstone Museum has
those of the local Blue Coat School of old', records Dr Clare. Girls at the Red
Maids' School, Bristol, founded as a charity by John Whitson (1558–1621) and
today an outstanding private day and boarding school still wear a red uniform
in modern style, but on Founders' Day and other special occasions revert to
the original uniform bonnet, tippet and apron over red dresses.

The Blue Coat boys' Tudor dress was copied by many later educational
foundations. When Dulwich College was established in 1619 by Edward
Alleyn, actor-manager and keeper of the King's Bear Garden, 12 poor
scholars were admitted free and, as Dr Clare records, were, by the original
Statute of Foundation, given, once a year at Easter, and oftener if needed,
'one surplice of white calico, one upper coat of good cloth and sad colour, the
bodice lined with canvas and the skirt with white cotton, one pair of drawers,
of white cotton, two canvas shirts with buckram bands to them, two pairs of
knit stockings, shoes as often as need shall require, two round bands, a girdle
and a black cap'.

A variation of this uniform was worn until 1857 – a long black coat with
soft turn-down collar and belt, and grey stockings. It is shown in a picture in the
Dulwich Picture Gallery of *Old time Tuition at Dulwich College*, 1828, by
J.F. Horsley, R.A. In 1857 uniform was discarded and all that was required
was 'a suitable cap or other mark of distinction'.

Boys at Colston's School in Bristol wore for many years a very picturesque uniform in the fashion of the year of its foundation, 1708, by Edward Colston, a governor of Christ's Hospital. It consisted of a long blue coat, partly lined in red, worn with blue breeches, red stockings, buckled shoes and a round hat trimmed with red ribbon and with a red tuft on top. A monument to the poet Thomas Chatterton, formerly in the church of St Mary Redcliffe, shows him in his school uniform, which was not changed to a newer style till 1873, then abolished in 1900. The Westminster Blue Coat School, founded in 1688, also wore the Tudor uniform, and a statue of a boy wearing it stands in a recess above the entrance, with the inscription: 'This is the Blew Coat School 1709'. Two similar statues stand by the font of St Bride's Church, off Fleet Street.

Sometimes the children of charity schools made their own clothes, and even spun the wool for them. The clothes allocation to each girl pupil at one school in the eighteenth century was 'a stuff gown, 2 linen bed gowns, 2 shifts, 2 pairs of gloves, 2 checked handkerchiefs, 2 blue aprons, two pair of stockings and one wolsey petticoat'. In 1708 the cost of such a uniform was quoted as 10s 3d for a girl and 9s 2d for a boy at a leading London charity school.

The prevalence of blue among these early uniforms is not accidental; blue dye was the cheapest and blue was traditionally the colour worn by servants, apprentices and other poor and humble groups. Freed of this humble connotation, it still remains a favourite choice for school uniforms, particularly those of girls, and the blue blazer is a proud garment for all ages. Further prestige and popularity among the young was given to blue by a quite different nineteenth-century development in children's costume – the immense and long-lasting vogue for sailor suits for boys and adaptations of the same attire for girls, which will be dealt with later. To cap all, there are today's universal blue jeans.

Although most of the records of early schoolboy dress relate to charity schools, they extend beyond that area in some cases; Eton for instance started as a charity school in 1462. Similar long gowns to those already described were worn there as the only uniform and also probably at other schools which either were or became public ones. They too originated as the normal boys' wear of the time. Some 1560 school bills survive with details of the clothing of the two sons of Sir William Cavendish, who went to Eton at the ages of ten and nine. They wore gowns of black frieze, which was the attire of oppidans as well as collegers for many years. They were hard on footwear, getting through seven pairs of shoes in a year. The long gowns, closed in front and fastened at neck and wrists, were 'not a mere adjunct to ordinary clothes intended to distinguish boys maintained by a royal or ecclesiastical foundation, but a real protection against the cold. The hood attached to it could be drawn over the head when necessary', says Hartley Kemball Cook in *Those Happy Days*.

Outside endowed schools uniforms did not begin to appear until the eighteenth century as a specific kind of youthful attire. A few glimpses of earlier children in the context of school do, however, throw some light on what they wore. There is a brief description of an ordinary Elizabethan schoolboy in one of the colloquies written by a Huguenot refugee schoolmaster, Claude Desainlieus, who taught at a school in St Paul's churchyard. He describes a young Londoner of the 'unwillingly to school' type getting ready to set out and demanding: 'Where have you layde my girdle and my inckehorne? Where are my sockes of linnen? Where is my cap, my mittaynes, my slippers, my handkarchif, my sachall, my penknife, my bookes?' It sounds unostentatious enough, but there is a different kind of schoolboy in the Lismore papers. The eldest boy of the family, Roger, was going off to board with a kinsman and to attend day school. He wore for winter a baize gown faced with fur, but for high days and holidays had a suit of ash-coloured satin, a doublet, hose, stockings with red garters and roses all to match, an embroidered girdle, a cloak of the same colour trimmed with squirrel fur. He had a taffeta ruff, and a sword fastened with a green scarf. He wore out five pairs of shoes a year – but died at ten years old, of a chill, so his grandeur did him little good.

A less affluent schoolboy emerges from a passage in the Verney letters of Stuart times, in which the boy writes: 'Mr Denton, the Taylor, have brought me a suite of closes of the same clothe that my cloke is off; he hath also brought me a sote with pair of upper stokings, and a paire of under reade stockings. . . . I doe lake some blacke rubin for to make me some cuffe strings and shoe strings. I have bought already one paire of each, but they are now almost worne out and therefore I shall take one paire of shoostrings against christmas, whether I goe to London or no. . . . It costeth me but a grote a yarde. I doe also take a hatt against christmas, for my oulde hatt which I have now is full of holes in the crowne of it.'

Another glimpse into clothing problems, in this case those of a girl, also comes in the Verney memoirs. An item of 1647 tells that a certain Miss Betty 'wants clothes from heade to foote, both woolen and linnen' – a plight familiar to the young at all times. Lady Verney suggests a £12 allowance a year, but explains: 'All heere keepes their daughters in silke. Ye doctor's wife ye other day made new silke gowns for all her daughters and I assure you Betty doth not pointe at wearing any other, and truly I cannot imagine which way you can keepe her in silke at thatt rate.' The child of the day was being decked out like a fashionable miniature adult in middle-class circles as well as among the aristocracy; socially the seventeenth-century doctor was not ranked very highly.

In 1685 another young Verney, Edward, going to Oxford at 16, wrote to his father: 'I want a Hatt and a payre of Fringed Gloves very much.' One hopes he got them; they were a happier contribution than that of a year or two later, when he was sent money for elaborate mourning for a brother and a box 'with a black Crepe Hatband, Black mourning Gloves, and Stockings and Shoe Buckles and 3 payres of black Buttons for wrist and neck.' Mourning was unfortunately a frequent infliction on the children of centuries when more than half those born died before the age of five and some half of the survivors before they were ten.

An early and highly picturesque reference to school uniforms which engages attention because it comes as a surprise and out of context occurs in *The Lives of the Norths*, already referred to. In the section dealing with the life of Dr John North, a brother of Lord Justice North and of the book's author, Roger North, the latter recalls that 'After the happy Restoration and while our doctor was

still at school, the master took occasion to publish his cavaliership by all the
ways he could contrive; and one was putting all the boarders who were of
the chief families in the country, into red cloaks, because the cavaliers about
the court usually wore such; and scarlet was commonly called the king's
colour. Of these he had near thirty parade before him through that town to
church; which made no vulgar appearance.' It must have been the most
picturesque as well as probably the earliest proud parade of school uniforms.

Girls could, however, claim a similar landmark in children's fashions. It
was not much later than this that pupils of Madame de Maintenon's school at
St Cyr, established in 1686, blossomed out into the first girls' school uniforms,
apart from those of charity schools. As her biographer, Charlotte Haldane,
describes them: 'They were divided into four groups charmingly and almost
coquettishly dressed in brown skirts and cloaks, their bodices stiffened by
whalebone, their white caps, collars and cuffs trimmed with lace, and ribbons
of various colours – blue for the eldest, then yellow, green and lastly red for
the littlest ones.' There were 300 staff and boarders at St Cyr, set up by
Madame de Maintenon, explains Mrs Haldane, 'for impoverished daughters
of the minor aristocracy, in similar circumstances to those of her own unhappy
youth, which was to become the model for the education of young French
women.'

Even in the eighteenth century school dress remained highly picturesque
and elegant. J.T. Smith in his *Book for a Rainy Day* recalls seeing the boys of
Mr Founteyne's boarding school crossing Marylebone High Street in his
youth: 'My youthful eyes were dazzled with the various colours of the dresses
of the youths, who walked two and two, some in pea green, others in sky
blue and several in the brightest scarlets; some of them wore gold laced hats,
while the flowing locks of others, at that time allowed to remain uncut in
schools, fell over their shoulders.' The future schoolboy was to look very
different from that.

3 First Reformers and First Fashions

Throughout the sixteenth, seventeenth and part of the eighteenth centuries children continued to be dressed as miniature adults in the recorded area of their attire – still mainly that of the high-born. Thus Elizabethan boys wore doublets, sleeveless jerkins, trunk hose and the breeches-length, balloon-shaped Venetians which are seen in many portraits, including that of the small James VI and I at the age of eight, in 1574. They wore the same silks, satins, brocades and velvets, feathered hats, neck ruffs as their fathers. Their underwear continued to be the universal shirt of linen or holland. Their fashions changed with those of adults, and were as much stiffened with buckram and padded with bombast as those of men. This style of dress continued until well into the seventeenth century, to about 1640.

Girls likewise followed their mothers and after the long but fairly simple dresses of very early years, went into adult-style farthingales and the long stiffened Elizabethan bodices, complete with stomachers and the whaleboned corsets of the time. Account books show that very rich materials, including brocades and velvets, were used. High ruffs were worn by girls not yet in their teens, but the very young seem to have been spared them. Heads were covered with caps indoors, sometimes small, decorative ones that covered little of the hair and were often made of silk or silver or gold thread. Stockings were usually of wool or cotton, knitted or shaped from fabric.

Fashion does not always change with the calendar, and these styles continued to be worn into the seventeenth century, but with a trend towards greater ease and freedom and less rigidity, thus echoing Royalist and Cavalier attitudes. For men and boys breeches first appeared briefly at the start of the century, but did not fully replace doublets and trunk and other styles of hose until about 1650. Large hats were worn by both men and boys, and from about 1640 boys began to wear wigs and to powder their hair in the adult style. Shaped coats with full skirts replaced the doublet about 1670, evolving from longer and looser versions of the doublet, and remained in fashion for boys until well into the eighteenth century; Girls followed their mothers closely into the era of panniers and, like them, continued to wear stiffened corsets and bodices, reaching to the under-arms but very short below the waist.

There was perhaps an unexpected degree of comfort in one garment mentioned frequently during these centuries – the nightgown. It was not, as we would expect, worn in bed or at night, but was an informal loose gown

18 James VI and I, aged eight, wears the fashionable man's Venetians, with a ruff and feathered cap

worn for warmth and comfort at any time. It was a kind of housecoat and is mentioned as being worn by both adults and children of both sexes from the sixteenth century. One, belonging to a sixteenth-century ten-year-old girl, is described in family accounts as being fur-trimmed, the cost of the fur being 10*d*. Nightgowns were often made of elaborate materials. A boy's rare eighteenth-century dressing gown, or banyan, in the Bath Museum, is of this character, in elaborately printed cotton.

19   The family of Arthur, 1st Baron Capel (1610–49). Some are dressed as elaborately as their parents, but the youngest members wear simpler clothes

There was still little evidence of children being recognized in their own right or of comfort and ease coming to their clothes – or to any fashionable clothes. Just how comfortable and practical ordinary children's attire could be is difficult to assess, but it was certainly not free in the uninhibited modern sense. The doctrine of original sin, the appalling severity of punishments and the pressure of intensive schooling also prevailed for centuries, inhibiting the idea of freedom for the young. In 1475 Mrs Agnes Paston wrote to her young son's tutor: 'If the boy has not done well, he will truly belash him till he will mend.' Lady Jane Grey's misfortunes included terror of her parents and misery whenever she was with them: 'For when I am in presence of either father or mother, whether I speak, keep silence, sit, stand or go, eat, drink, be merry or sad, be sewing, playing, dancing or doing anything else, I must do it as it were in such weight, measure and number, even as perfectly as god made the world, or else I am so sharply taunted, so cruelly threatened, yet, presently sometimes with pinches, nips and bobs, and some ways which I will not name for the horror I bear them, so without measure misordered, that I think myself in hell.' John Wesley's mother not only beat her children regularly, to drive sin out of them, but even intimidated them, from the age of one year, into

20 Less rigid, but still very
elaborate fashions for small girls
in the seventeenth century, seen
in this portrait of about 1670 by
John Richard Wright

crying only quietly while suffering this. Such a system gave the child no
chance of having his rights recognized and no chance therefore of having a
say in what he wore, which was one symbol of such an acknowledgment.

Change, however, had been on its way for a long time, though it took
centuries for it to have practical effect. Unlike changes in adult fashions it
did not come from the children concerned, who still and for long afterwards

had no say in what they wore. Nor was it brought about by fashion leaders, or by the assertive class-consciousness which traditionally underlies the introduction of new, exclusive fashions by the dominant class in a society.

The impetus behind the liberation of children's dress lay right outside the fashion world. It was the result of the efforts of enlightened teachers and educationalists who for generations had been inveighing against repressive attitudes to children, reflected in, among other things, their clothes. Such efforts had often little immediate effect, but they bore fruit eventually.

Erasmus (1466–1536) wrote a treatise on the liberal eduction of boys, urging that teaching should never become tedious and should be adapted to the capacity of the young mind and to the training of the young memory. He also advocated education of a similar kind for girls. Ascham's *The Schoolmaster* (1570) urged gentle methods of love rather than fear in education. Sir Thomas Elyot, who wrote copiously on education in Tudor times, also urged tenderness and opposed violence to the young.

The subject of children's clothing was taken seriously by early reformers, mainly because of its effect on the health and physical welfare of the young. Thus Edward Mulcaster, the first headmaster of Merchant Taylors' school from 1581 to 1586 and then high master of St Paul's until 1608, urged in his book on the training of young children that clothing should be warm and light. Unfortunately in this respect the greatest of Elizabethan educationalists had little practical effect at the time. Dr Almond of Loretto, also in the seventeenth century, urged a freer, more hygienic way of bringing up children and was an advocate of bare-headedness (then revolutionary), as well as of active play, physical exercise and no eating between meals. Endymion Porter,

21   Although their clothes remain formal, the Graham children, by Hogarth (1697–1764) are in happy mood, as if in anticipation of future freedom

22   Boy's doublet and breeches, 1649–50, look almost comfortable

23   Boy's shirt, early eighteenth century with elaborate embroidery

a notable courtier (1587–1649), writing home to his wife from one of his frequent inevitable absences on official duties, seems to have given heed to the reformers, because he advised her to let little George, their eldest boy, play bareheaded out of doors, 'else you will have him constantly sick'.

Hannah Woolley in *The Gentlewoman's Companion* (1675) condemned the wearing of tight corsets by young girls and attacked mothers and nurses who, 'by cloistering you up in a steel or whalebone prison, open a door to Consumption with many other dangerous inconveniences, as Crookedness, for Mothers striving to have their Daughters small in the middle, do pluck and draw their bones away.' More than 200 years later the same protest was still being voiced loudly.

The first effective supporter of children's rights was Komensky (1592–1671), writing in German but soon translated into English to make a big impact on educationalists in Britain. This was increased when, during the Thirty Years' War, he spent several years in England after being driven out of his native Moravia. He knew Milton, John Evelyn, Lord Herbert, all of whom were interested in children's education and inclined to new views. He was a pioneer in advising following nature in child training and in this respect the forerunner of Froebel, Pestalozzi and of the kindergarten system in general.

His greatest importance, however, lay in the extent to which he influenced John Locke, whose *Thoughts Concerning Education*, published in 1693, 40 years later, was the real start of a revolution in the whole conception of children's clothing as well as of their general upbringing. Locke, who anticipated Rousseau by half a century and influenced him profoundly, urged, in face of constricting prevailing fashions, that children's clothing should not be too warm, heavy or tight. He advocated cold baths and, oddly, that the feet should not be too well shod nor carefully kept dry, but that thin, leaky shoes should be worn so as to accustom the child to wet feet and therefore harden him. He too advocated hatlessness and open air activities. Locke's view found a sympathizer in America in William Penn who, in a letter to his wife in the early years of the eighteenth century, not long after Locke's book, declared that 'children had rather be making of tools and instruments of play, shaping, drawing, framing and building than getting by heart some rules of propriety of speech, and those would also follow with more judgment and less trouble and time.' This was 50 years before Rousseau caught the attention of the western world with his assertion of the child's right to freedom and his need for it.

The influence of Locke was probably greater than that of Rousseau, even though it was the latter who captured the limelight and has been hailed by posterity as the liberator of the child. Many of Rousseau's reforms, put forward in 1762 in *Emile*, had been anticipated by Locke, to whom he acknowledged his debt, and had in fact also been voiced by others and in some cases adopted. *Emile*, however, was an instant best-seller, was rapidly translated into English in two versions in 1763, was praised and banned and was notorious and controversial.

The reason, as ever, was that the time was ripe for it. *Emile* was the children's charter, dealing not only with general ways of bringing up children but also, very fully, with their clothes, and it was from about this time that children's clothing began to have its own identity. That this should be so was an intrinsic part of the new tenderness in public attitudes to children. 'Love childhood', says Rousseau, in contrast to what previous generations had seemed to feel, 'indulge its sports, its pleasures, its delightful instincts. Who has not sometimes regretted that age when laughter was ever on the lips and when the heart was ever at peace?' This concern was, as a recent commentator has said, 'something quite new, especially his assertion that childhood has a right to happiness, that it is an independent state and not simply an ante-room to maturity.' It was new so far as general acceptance was concerned and it went further than any previous reforms had done.

On clothes and fashion Rousseau's rules for Emile are specific. He is to live out of doors, to be allowed to run, even to fall. 'Emile shall have no head-pads [that is, the pudding], no go-cart [a kind of frame long used to assist walking], no leading strings. . . . The limbs of a growing child should be free to move easily in his clothes; nothing should cramp their growth or move-ment; there should be nothing tight, nothing fitting closely to the body, no belt of any kind. The French style of dress, uncomfortable and unhealthy for a man, is especially bad for children. The stagnant humours, whose circulation is interrupted, putrify in a state of inaction. . . . The hussar's dress [a contem-porary fashion], far from correcting this fault, increases it, and compresses the whole of the child's body. . . . The best plan is to keep children in frocks as long as possible and then to provide them with loose clothes, without trying to define the shape which is only another way of distorting it. Their defects of body and mind may all be traced to the same source, the desire to make men of them before their time.'

24 Boy's suit, early eighteenth century, the kind of formal fashion that was soon to give way to a new simplicity

He goes on to be more specific. 'There are bright colours and dull, children like the bright colours best, and they suit them better too.' Materials should not, however, be chosen because they are rich, for this means that the children's 'hearts are already given over to luxury, to every caprice of fashion, and this taste is certainly not their own' – the first suggestion that children know best what they should wear. Comfort is to be sought in clothes; 'before the child is enslaved by our prejudices his first wish is always to be comfortable. The plainest and most comfortable clothes, those which leave him most liberty, are what he always likes best.'

Clothes should be light-weight for active children. 'Emile should wear little or nothing on his head all the year round', so as to strengthen the bones of the skull, so 'accustom your children to go bareheaded winter and summer, day and night.' Of Locke, whom in general he much admired, Rousseau had only one criticism to make: why did he advocate leaky shoes on health grounds, yet at the same time say that children ought not to lie on damp grass? Of Rousseau in general posterity has one major criticism: why did the first great liberator of the child abandon five of his own children (incidentally

25   Before the change: a Court dress for a twelve-year-old girl, about 1740, in cream ribbed silk with a floral and trellis design. There are wide panniers, as in women's fashions, but she carries her doll

26   Towards simplicity: Two Little Miss Edgars, by Arthur Devis (1711–87)

illegitimate) in a Paris foundling hospital? He claimed that to write his books *and* support them was impossible and that therefore it was for their own good.

The revolution in children's clothes is generally dated from round about 1770, four years after Rousseau, a fugitive from France because of his religious views, had spent some months in England. The liberation which so many people had sought for so long became a reality, but it did not happen overnight and for some considerable time both old and new styles of dressing children co-existed. That was to be expected, because the change in dressing was part of a social change. 'The earliest record of a definite costume for children is about 1770 or 1775', says Iris Brooke in her book *English Children's Costume since 1775*. 'Before that children were dressed in exactly the same manner as their parents.' F. Gordon Roe in *The Georgian Child* agrees that 'it is from the '70s that the slow emergence of the modern child may be traced, for it is reasonable to suggest that the youngsters brought up and dressed in the likeness of their elders may have "grown up" more quickly

27   New-style fashions for girls in a water-colour drawing made at Windsor about 1760, by Paul Sandby, R.A. It shows the three daughters of the 2nd Earl of Waldegrave, with Miss Keppel, daughter of the Bishop of Exeter

than they would otherwise have done.' The reverse side of the argument, that grown-ups were relaxing and becoming addicted to childlike fun, is suggested in his next sentence: 'In contrast, a good many Georgian adults possessed a strong streak of childishness which often took the form of horse-play.' It is a point which will become relevant later in the story of children's clothes as an influence on adult fashions.

Phillis Cunnington and Anne Buck state that 'until the 1780s, a boy, once he was breeched, was dressed in a small replica of his father's coat, waistcoat and breeches', and, again, 'knee breeches were worn by all boys until the 1780s', but this date, surely, is too late. R. Turner Wilcox, the American costume expert, is on the other hand premature in placing the change in children's attire as early as the first decade of the eighteenth century. Doris Langley Moore, who has researched the subject in depth, finds a record of the new girls' dresses in a portrait of about 1750 in the collection of Viscountess Lee of Fareham. Iris Brooke refers to Sir Joshua Reynolds' portrait of the little Viscount Althorp as the first example in painting of the new-style boy's suit and dates it in the 1770s, suggesting that it 'may probably claim to be the earliest record of children's costume', that is of a style distinct from that of adults. This, however, is wrong; the portrait is that of the boy who later became 3rd Earl Spencer, notable Parliamentarian and Chancellor of the Exchequer, and it was painted in 1786, when he was aged four. R.T. Wilcox in *The Mode in Costume* says that 'a portrait of Marie Antoinette with her two children, painted in 1785 by Wertmuller, portrays the Dauphin in long trousers and a short buttoned jacket with a frill at the open neck. The little girl wears a simple frock of English style, also with a frill at the low round neck and a sash about the waist.'

Exact dates may sometimes be in doubt, but what is certain is that the change was gradual: 'Years passed before boys in the new-fangled dress ceased to be conspicuous', says F. Gordon Roe, and miniature adults co-existed with new-look children for a considerable time at the end of the eighteenth century. The significant point about the change is that the distinctive children's clothes which now appeared bore no relation to what adults were wearing. It was the first time this had happened, a unique event in costume history. Doris Langley Moore has called it 'the great sartorial event of the eighteenth century', and that is no exaggeration. It was not only great but also unusual in its nature. It was the first time comfort and convenience had been the basis of any fashion, at least in the present cycle of history. It was a curious portent that children, hitherto condemned to follow adults in the wearing of uncomfortable fashions, should have taken the lead in the fashion liberation that was not to become general until the present century.

Little boys, though they still wore dresses for the first few years of their lives, now did so for a shorter time, often less than four years. When the 'breeching' stage was reached, they no longer went into the fitted knee breeches, skirted coats, long waistcoats, tricorne hats and elaborate accessories of their elders. Instead they adopted trousers, an item of wear hitherto limited to countrymen, labourers and sailors, unknown in polite society and not to be worn by men for more than a generation to come. Ankle-length or slightly above the ankle, tight at first but later looser, these trousers were

28 John Charles, Viscount Althorp, 1786, later 3rd Earl of Spencer, aged four, a leader in the new children's fashions, who was later to be leader of the House of Commons and a noted statesman. Portrait by Sir Joshua Reynolds

usually made of nankeen or other cotton materials. With them small boys wore simple, soft shirts of white lawn or cotton, sometimes with soft frills at the low, comfortable necklines, like Viscount Althorp. This is a superb example of the new-style boy's dress, what was called the 'skeleton suit', at its most charming – easy and comfortable and, apart from the sash and hat, it could belong to today. The hair is short and uncurled, the shoes, with small buckles, could belong to our own times. Shirts were usually buttoned on to the trousers above the waist. Sashes were not always worn, but if so were in contrasting colours, pastel or bright. Short, simple jackets were also added, as warmth required. The colours of these skeleton suits tended to be pastels or white. Buckled shoes in the current style were worn at first, but soon were replaced by the end of the century with soft, simple pumps. Wide-rimmed, low-crowned hats, country-style and of straw or felt according to the season, were also worn. Hair was short or shoulder-length and hung naturally. The Bethnal Green Museum of Childhood has two such suits, one for a tiny boy in cream nankeen with a short jacket; the other, for a seven or eight year old, has cutaway tails and is shown with a wide-brimmed black hat.

This style of boy's dress, with no affinity to anything that had preceded it in the story of fashion, continued to be worn by small boys for the next thirty years or more. Jane Austen, in a letter of 1801, asks for a pattern of 'the jacket

29 Little boys wore the new-style dresses, like those of girls, in their early years. Here Lord Willoughby de Broke and his family show the new fashions about 1770

30 The skeleton suit in an 1801 print

and trousers, or whatever it is that Elizabeth's boys wear when they are first put into breeches'. The skeleton suit was widely shown in portraits from the 1770s, notably those of Reynolds, Romney, Gainsborough and Raeburn. These portraits, unlike previous ones of children, are almost invariably relaxed, casual and happy, They show children at ease, often with their pet animals, in country settings, smiling with health and happiness in an apparently endless sunny summer. The wearing of such clothes in portraits shows that they were well established; that was the way parents wanted their sons to be recorded and remembered. The glow of health and the bright summer are less realistic and the death rate among children remained terribly high. But the existence of these portraits in such numbers is a strong testimony to the recognition of the child as an individual in his own right. Such recognition had still far to go in understanding the child or, more accurately, in endeavouring to understand him, but its emergence at this time is significant.

It would be reasonable to expect such a revolution in children's dress to be well documented and its history clearly recorded, but in fact it is wrapped in obscurity. No one has succeeded in tracing its origins or even its exact course. One tradition has it that this kind of suit was introduced by Marie Antoinette for her son as part of the mock simplicity which turned her court into a kind of make-believe Arcadia, peopled by milk-maids, shepherds and shepherdesses. Elizabeth McClellan, in her *History of American Costume*, says that 'Marie Antoinette was the first mother to disregard the established court fashion. She had a simple suit of jacket and trousers made for the Dauphin, but the *Chronicle of Fashion* assures us that "even this, probably the most sensible of all the ill-fated Queen's innovations in dress, was reviled as if the paraphernalia

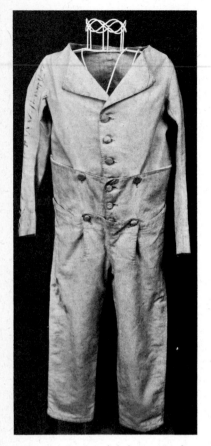

31 An actual skeleton suit of the early nineteenth century, from the Bethnal Green Museum of Childhood

32 *Family Group in a Land* by F. Wheatley (1747–1801 shows easy clothes for the children, but formality for ladies

of full dress was a moral obligation".' Another view is that French dressmakers, endeavouring to interpret Rousseau's not very explicit instructions
about children's dress, invented a kind of basic boiler-suit, with a shirt whose
ruffles were a concession to their smart customers. Ackermann shows such a
suit among his many pictures of children's dress of the early nineteenth century.

The common factor in the various explanations is that the new dress was
accepted as rural in origin. Country life was still the norm for most people
and upper-class children were likely to wear for everyday life clothes similar
to those of ordinary village youngsters whose pursuits and games they would,
like children everywhere, share to some degree. Rousseau's back-to-nature
movement turned to the country for its life-style, starting with children,
and in the subsequent Romantic movement children were of great significance.
Stuart Maxwell and Robin Hutchinson in their *Scottish Costume* make the point
that 'not only the children but the working class led the way in adopting the
nineteenth-century fashions, while the upper classes held on longer to the
eighteenth-century styles. . . . It was a levelling-up of fashion, not down as
previously.' They also record a parallel to the Marie Antoinette theory of
children's dress in the fact that Sir Walter Scott's family was painted by
Sir David Wilkie in 1815 'in the garb of rustic peasants' in a group now in
the Scottish National Portrait Gallery. His daughters were similarly recorded
in rustic dress. The famous author was very much on the *qui-vive* socially
and in this painting he was being true to the fashion of his day.

Trousers, a development from the old-time braies of Anglo-Saxon men
and boys, were still worn by countrymen and their sons. When the idea of
free, easy clothing for boys was mooted, trousers were there, ready to be
given a new status and eventually to become general wear for men of all

33   The first boiler suit for a
small boy in an Ackermann
print of 1810. The smaller child
wears a simple dress

34   Free and easy trousers for
small boys at play

35   The Blunt Children, by Zoffany, show the new simple dresses worn about 1770 in a fashionably rural setting

classes on all occasions. It was natural that small boys, having grown used to the comfort of the skeleton suit, should continue to wear its trousers when they were not so small and be reluctant to change to the discomfort of breeches. As the rise of industry and commerce made practical clothing necessary for men and as the city gentleman superseded the courtier and leisured aristocrat as the norm of society, peacock fashions for men disappeared and the trouser suit became general wear.

That men should have reversed all tradition and not only followed their young sons in donning trousers but also adopted a fashion that came from the bottom and not the top of the social scheme of things was perhaps prophetic of things to come. At any rate it happened and developed gradually. From the 1790s men's breeches acquired extensions, like later riding breeches. With the French Revolution, which made traditional elegance perilous to the wearer, men in France and then elsewhere took to wearing long, pantaloon-style nether garments, strapped under the ankles or worn under high boots. Stockinette tights reaching to just above the ankle were a later move out of the formality of breeches towards the trousers which, after spreading from younger to older boys, became general wear for men in the second quarter of the nineteenth century.

Meantime, in the second part of the eighteenth century, girls began to share in the young liberation movement and were freed from their stiff, tightly fitted silks and satins, their cage-like full skirts and their occasional full-scale panniers. They also ceased, though only for a time, to wear the tight, constricting stays which had accompanied those adult fashions. Instead, they began to wear simple, straight dresses of lawn, muslin and various fine cottons, with easy necklines, tiny sleeves and soft sashes at unrestricted waists. Colours, as with the boys, were soft and usually pale, with a preference for white, at least for best. The white party dress, which was to be the young girl's wear for more than 150 years and almost until our own time, had arrived, and it was to have a near-continuous history.

The origins of this style of dress, as in the case of the skeleton suit, are not clear. It seems most likely to be a continuation of the dress worn by babies and very young children of both sexes and to have been retained for slightly older girls as part of the cult of simplicity largely inspired by Rousseau, even though he did not include girls among his young Utopians in *Emile*. This is supported by the fact that small boys, before being breeched, also wore this type of dress, seen as early as about 1767 in Zoffany's painting of the Blunt children, in which two small boys wear low-necked, simple white dresses with blue sashes, and short hair. It may also, like the boys' attire of the same time, have had links with traditional simple country clothes worn by humble rural people, and therefore attractive to fashion when it was set on a 'back-to-nature' course. What is significant is the extreme simplicity of everything the small girl wore. Skirts rose a few inches above the ankles. Calico petticoats, sometimes coloured, were worn under the new-style dresses, and were particularly important when, as often, the dresses were of transparent materials. Fichus sometimes filled in the necklines. Little jackets, spencer-style, and shoulder-capes, called tippets, were worn over the dresses for warmth. Hats were simple round styles, sometimes tied down with ribbons to form a kind of bonnet, and mob caps were also worn, alone – or under the hats. But girls, like boys, were often bareheaded. Hair could be long, or shoulder-length, or cropped short – a new fashion at the turn of the century, when small girls had boy-style short hair. The Bethnal Green Museum has several examples of these dresses, slim, very simple, one of transparent gauze with a lining. They have little puff sleeves and drawstrings under the arms and are dated as early nineteenth century. An earlier example in the Victoria and Albert Museum is much fuller, with a *bouffant* skirt.

The changes in the appearance of little girls at this time is summed up by Dorothy Margaret Stuart in *The Girl Through the Ages*: From the mid-eighteenth century, she says: 'No longer were infants tortured with whalebone stays and padded petticoats; the baby sister of the sculptor Flaxman has a roomy, easy frock, and the engaging child in Walton's *Fruit Barrow* wears a simple white dress with a shady blue hat, though her pretty mama boasts an uptilted hat nodding with plumes, and a tight-waisted gown encumbered with vast panniers. The Augustan girl-child, as painted by the great artists of the time, is a real child, with her locks unfrizzed, with a loose frock, usually white, and no finery more gorgeous than an azure ribbon or a pair of coral-coloured shoes. Sometimes she wore a prim little cape of black silk, as Princess Sophia does in Hoppner's portrait of her; sometimes she has a fur-trimmed tippet and muff, like the small daughter of the Duke of Buccleuch whose portrait by Reynolds charmed Horace Walpole so much.'

This trend continued. There is a charming description of the little daughters of George III and Queen Charlotte with their parents on the terrace at Windsor Castle: 'The golden-haired, muslin-clad princesses who fluttered round them like a cloud of white butterflies were as pretty a vision as ever

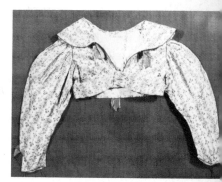

36 Child's spencer, 1825–30, at the Bethnal Green Museum of Childhood

those grey walls beheld.' Fanny Burney tells of the tiny Princess Amelia (1783–1810) walking on that same terrace at the age of three 'in a robe coat covered with fine muslin, a dressed close cap, white gloves and a fan.'

As with boys, these small girls' new fashions anticipated those to be worn by their elders a generation later. Stuart Maxwell and Robin Hutchinson again sum up what happened.

'The new style is seen first in children's dress. Little girls in portraits from the 1780s on have white, low-necked, high-waisted dresses, the necks round at first and then square. Their skirts are full, but they fall straight to ankle length. By the '90s the skirts are not so full, the neck is always square, cut below the very short puff sleeves, and the waist is always marked by a coloured sash. In the early years of the century, girls had short, boyish-looking haircuts, and in their simple dresses reaching to the middle of the calf, their white stockings and their low-heeled slipper-like shoes, they must have enjoyed a freedom which had not been the lot of children for many years. They were to lose that freedom as the century progressed.'

About the time of the French Revolution, a great if temporary leveller, women made a complete break with the elaborate fashions they had worn for centuries and they too sought freedom, which was the mood of the time, in simple cotton and muslin dresses in much the same styles as those already being worn by their small daughters. The materials were not, however, completely new. Muslins and gauzes had for a time been part of their fashions, the fabrics part of the growing trade of Europe with the East and especially with India. Light, beautiful muslins and silks of this kind had at first been very expensive, and therefore greatly attractive to high fashion from the seventeenth century. In the next century such muslins were being produced in Britain by the growing cotton trade, already centred on Manchester. The raw materials came from Asia Minor, the Orient and the East Indies, but factory manufacture brought prices down to a generally acceptable level and the boom in simplicity could be met. A further coincidental factor in moving fashion towards this new simplicity was the fact that soft, airy draperies were thought to have an affinity with classical robes as seen in statues being brought to light by excavations started in 1760 at Herculaneum. Thus the appeal of the Greek world to the idealism fostered by the French Revolution, the growth of trade and the first ever 'youth explosion' all conspired, by an incongruous amalgam, to change the course of fashion, with children at the heart of it all.

4 Real-life Recollections of Eighteenth Century Children's Dress

Fortunately for posterity the first children's fashions, in the 60-odd years before photography took over recording them, were remarkably fully described and discussed in a wealth of memoirs and children's books. The latter were a new development, another sign of the new attention being given to children, and many of them still make fascinating reading.

Heralded by *Robinson Crusoe*, published in 1719, the children's book trade was first established on an appreciable scale by John Newbery, who settled in London in 1744 and published over 200 books for children – books for enjoyment and not, as in the past, for moral and didactic purposes only. Prominent among these books was Sarah Fielding's *The Governess*, for long popularly known as *Mrs Teachem* from the name of the schoolmistress upon whose school it was centred. It was published in 1749 and within a few months had gone into the first of a constant series of new editions extending well into Victorian times. It has even recently been reissued. It was not only the first known full-length original story book for children, the first 'school story' and the first to deal with ordinary children and everyday things, but it also was the work of a zealous follower of Locke and in many ways it anticipated Rousseau, being published 13 years before *Emile*. Like Locke, Sarah hated cruelty to children, especially corporal punishment. She advocated freedom and kindness – and was early in urging simplicity in dress. One of the pupils, Miss Nancy Spruce, is addicated to 'fine ribands and laced caps' and is criticized for this vanity; when naughty she is made to wear 'an old Stuff Coat' as punishment. Further disapproval of the then prevalent elaborate dress of girls is voiced in the first fictional description of girls' dress of the day, also in *The Governess*. This is given when Lady Caroline and Lady Fanny Delun, 'who had previously known Miss Jenny Peace', another pupil at Mrs Teachem's school, come to visit her. Lady Caroline, aged 14, 'tall and genteel, was dressed in a Pink Robe, embroider'd thick with Gold, and adorned with very fine Jewels, and the finest *Mechlin* lace. . . . Her fingers were in perpetual Motion, either adjusting her Tucker, placing her Plaits of her Robe, or fiddling with a Diamond Cross that hung down her Bosom.' Lady Fanny's dress was plain red, 'but she kept looking in the mirror all the time.'

When Mrs Sherwood (1775–1851) produced her plagiarized version of *The Governess* in 1820, she described the clothes of the pupils at Mrs Teachem's in the new simpler style which by then had been established. When taken

37   Schoolboy dress seen in
*'Black Monday' or the Departure
for School*, 1790, engraved after
W. Bigg

out walking on Saturday afternoons the girls were 'each in a silk slip, with a lawn apron and lace tucker, and wearing a small cap with a narrow border of lace neatly quilted round it. Each of the young ladies had a rosebud and a sprig of jessamine in her bosom, and each held in her hand a silk hood and tippet, ready to put on as soon as their governess should appear.' The frontispiece shows dresses with the high waists, short sleeves and low necks which began in the late eighteenth century, the skirts reaching to above the ankles and edged with a narrow frill; the whole outfit in the Kate Greenaway style. It was a recognizable version of the new mode of girls' dressing, which was established and had taken on some variety by then.

Just as *The Governess* was a best-seller cherished by generations of girls and one of the longest-lived of all children's stories, so that Mrs Teachem became a household word, likewise *The History of Sandford and Merton*, by Thomas Day, published in three parts nearly 40 years later, in 1787–9, became a prime favourite of generations of boys. Though basically a good story, it is also full of Rousseau-like ideas of health, equality and the nature-cult. It is the first treatise on socialism for the young, the schoolboy's Burns and Wordsworth – and it is still very readable, very human in its appeal, endearing in its trustful moral code, despite a lot of priggishness. Thomas Day was a fervent disciple of Rousseau and, under the influence of Richard Edgeworth, father of that other disciple, Maria, campaigned in his writings against what he considered a decadent and trivial society. He brought up an orphan, Sabrina Sidney, on the lines of Rousseau's Sophie, but later came round to the view that the social and civilized man and not the 'natural' one was the ideal to be sought.

Tommy Merton, the rich six year old whose conversion to the virtues of the simple, honest life is the theme of the book, starts as a spoiled child 'taught to sit still for fear of spoiling his clothes, and to stay in the house for fear of injuring his complexion' – like so many children of that and previous times. He has a fine waistcoat, white stockings and wears breeches – showing that the change-over to the new skeleton suit was gradual. Harry Sandford, the farmer's son chosen to share his teaching and instrumental to his reform, is plainly dressed. When, at the end of the book, Tommy repents of his former ways the symbol of his reform is his decision to wear plain clothes: 'He had demolished the elegance of his curls; he had divested his dress of every appearance of finery, every article of his attire was plain and simple. Thus habited, he appeared so totally changed from what he had been, that even his mother . . . could not help exclaiming . . . "You look more like a ploughboy than a young gentleman". "Mama", answered Tommy very gravely, "I am now only what I ought always to have been . . . I have bidden farewell to dress and finery for ever".' There is an accompanying illustration of the new Tommy in smock and plain breeches. It was part of the revolution in childhood.

In Mrs Sherwood's *The Fairchild Family*, written in 1811–16, published in 1818, and another foremost classic of children's literature, little Henry is 'in pinafores', but also wears white trousers and a petticoated jacket, and is promised a boy's cloth jacket by his mother. He was then not quite eight. He objected to wearing a shawl because it made him like a girl. The petti-coated jacket was an anticipation of the later tunic which in various forms became another distinctive item of boys' wear. An 1830 fashion plate shows a boy with a long tunic coat with a belt, light trousers, a top hat and long hair.

When in 1853 Susan Sibbald at the age of 70 started her eight-year-long stint of writing her reminiscences of her early life at the request of one of her nine sons, she did not intend these annals of the 1780s and 1790s for publication. It was not till 1926 that one of the most vivid, human and detailed records of a childhood at the end of the eighteenth century in a prosperous, happy, middle-class family was edited by her great grandson and finally published. In it her pen pictures of how she and her seven sisters looked come out of the printed page sharp and clear as in life. They lived in the schoolroom 'except of an evening, when we had to be dressed out for the occasion, in color'd silk slips and thin muslin frocks, which were very suitable, as the moment we entered the drawing room, after our formal curtsies, we had to sit up all in a row, and as we were constantly told "be silent, and look pretty, as children should be seen and not heard".' (Susan spent her last years in Canada and used the American spelling of certain words.)

Muslin dresses were generally worn for best. When Susan was at boarding school at Bath a big occasion was 'our Ball', for which 'we were all to be dressed in book-muslin frocks, with primrose color'd sashes wide and long, and wreaths of roses of the same color on our heads, which might be had at Mrs Somebody's on Milsom Street.' It was a grand occasion, held at 'the Rooms'. There was on the other hand a minor disaster when, arriving at school at Bath, she went to get a white frock only to find that crayons had been packed with her clothes and 'lo and behold, there were almost all my nice new clothes, stained with red, blue, yellow and green chalks.' Washing, however, put them right, further evidence of the prevalence of muslins and cottons in the young wardrobe at the turn of the century.

She gives many other glimpses into the life of schoolgirls at the time. On Sunday 'we all were dressed in white frocks.' She had a drawer at school 'to keep my gloves, sashes and frills in.' The girls wore dressing gowns: at night 'the first thing to be done after going to our rooms, was to take off our frocks, hang them up, and put on our dressing gowns.' Schoolboys, including the later Tom Brown, did not have this luxury. The girls led active lives; 'being Summer at 4 o'clock bonnets, spencers, or tippets, and walking shoes on, we were paired off two and two, and took a walk into the country.' She wants new shoes and describes 'a pair of black morocco shoes bound with Coqlicot' (a bright scarlet, the 'colour of the blazing Comet geranium'), for which the shoemaker comes to measure her.

The fashion at this time by which women wore a costume closely modelled on the riding habit for travelling was also followed by teenage girls, according to another passage. Setting off for Scotland with one of her sisters, Susan recalls: 'I can well remember how smart I thought we looked in our hats and feathers, habits with lapels which when opened displayed waistcoats, frilled habit shirts, stand up collars and black silk handkerchiefs round our necks, so that to look at us through the windows of the carriage if it were not for the feathers and curls, we might have been taken for two youths.'

That the childish muslin dresses were by that time also worn by grown-ups is recorded. Her older sister Mary comes 'to say farewell to the schoolroom, and oh! how pretty we thought her dress, white book muslin over a pink silk slip, a long and broad sash and bows on her sleeves of the same color, but we could not but grieve to see her beautiful brown hair powdered.' It is a perfect Gainsborough portrait. White dresses were also worn for Queen Charlotte's Ball and for 'a great dinner' when she was newly grown-up Children also still wore them; she describes a niece of five years old about 1806: 'I think I can see her now in a white frock and red morocco shoes, which children then wore, come dancing into the room' – a poignant little recollection, for the child died soon afterwards, from convulsions caught by eating green apples in the Glen.

Moving slightly further on, more vivid word pictures of children of the first years of the nineteenth century come from the brilliant pen of another grandmother, also writing for her own family and not for publication. The most detailed on-the-spot descriptions of girls' dress at this time are contained in the *Memoirs of a Highland Lady*, the superbly realistic, detailed and sometimes harrowing story of her early days written by Elizabeth Grant of Rothiemurchus during the last 40 years of her long life (1797–1885) for her own children and a niece, and published after her death on the initiative of one of her daughters.

In the Highlands, where much of their time was spent, the children were, thankfully, allowed to run wild out of doors, and freedom extended to dress, because their nurse in 1800 'dressed us often after a fashion.' This nurse, a widow, Mrs Herbert, had incidentally, a son 'in the blue-coat school; he was now and then allowed to come and see his mother in his curious dress – the queer, petticoat coat and yellow stockings.' Less manly, perhaps, than the family child, Jane, who always put on her spencers and pinafores the wrong way to make believe they were jackets, 'because she really was a boy in all her tastes'.

Mrs Grant's description of the torture of the morning icy bath is a classic in child mismanagement, but after it the children were 'taken to the house-keeper's room, which was always warm, to be dried; there we dressed, without any flannel, and in cotton frocks with short sleeves and low necks'. For evenings they went down to dinner 'in full dress, like the footmen', and that meant white frocks. In 1807, in mourning for Uncle Leitch, 'our white frocks were decorated with black crape sashes, the long tails of which did charmingly for playing at horses.' On a visit to Duffus, to Sir Archibald and Lady Dunbar and their children, she recalls that 'Ellen and Margaret Dunbar wore sashes with their white frocks, and had each a pair of silk stockings, which they drew on for full dress, a style that much surprised me, as I, at home or abroad, had only my pink gingham frocks for the morning, white calico for the afternoon, cotton stockings at all times, and not a ribbon, a curl, or an ornament about me.'

Once, in London, a sudden treat came her way: 'I was to dress as quick as possible in my best white frock to go to the Opera. How old was I that happy night? – thirteen within a week or two. My dress was a plain white frock with plenty of tucks, a little embroidery at the waist, white calico long gloves and a cropped head, the hair brushed bright with oil, which to me made the toilette complete.'

In 1814, when she was reckoned to be grown up and new dresses were planned for her, she looked back on her accustomed wear: 'My sisters and I had hitherto been all dressed alike. In summer we wore pink gingham or nankin frocks in the morning, white in the afternoon. Our common bonnets were of coarse straw lined with green, and we had tippets to all our frocks. The best bonnets were of finer straw, lined and trimmed with white, and we had silk spencers of any colour that suited my mother's eye. In the winter we wore dark stuff frocks, black and red for a while – the intended mourning for the king. At night always scarlet stuff with bodices of black velvet and bands of the same at the hem of the petticoat. While in England our wraps were in pelisse form and made of cloth, with beaver bonnets, the bonnets did in the Highlands, but on outgrowing the pelisses they were replaced by cloaks with hoods, made of tartan . . . the red dress tartan of our clan . . . Our habits were made of the green tartan'.

The grown-up dresses to which she was promoted were not very different. They had frills and tucks and flounces and embroidery and were made in coloured gingham, cambric and muslin. But they were young girl dresses,

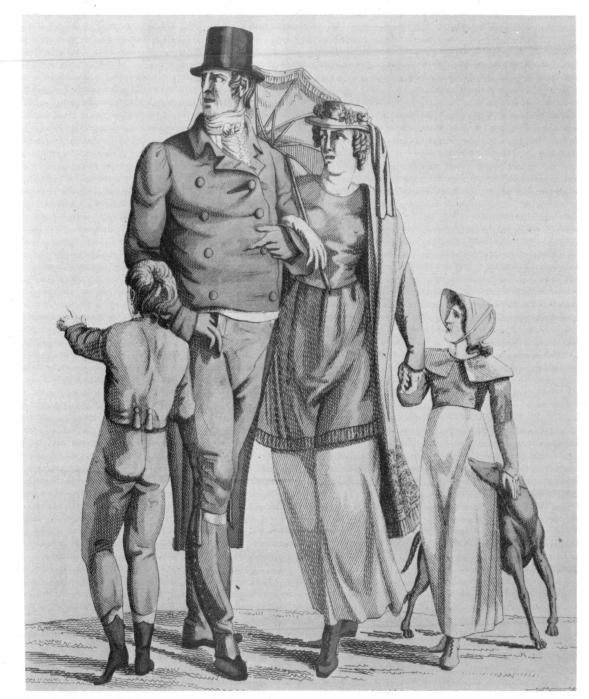

38   Fashions of 1816 shown in a
fashion plate *La Famille
Anglaise à Paris*, the boy in the
skeleton suit and the girl with
tippet and straw bonnet as
described by Mrs Grant

with more affinity to the schoolroom ones than to those of older women. In London her mother wore velvet, satin and rich silks, but Elizabeth had 'nets, gauzes, Roman-pearl trimmings and French wreaths with a few substantial morning and dinner dresses.' The first teenage fashions, perhaps.

Dressed-up children are continually recorded. Fanny Price in Jane Austen's *Mansfield Park* fears that her grand cousins 'could not but hold her cheap when they found she had but two sashes and had never learned French.' Later, the ten-year-old Jane Eyre, spending Christmas with her cousins at Gateshead Hall in the early nineteenth century, found that her share of the festivities 'consisted in witnessing the daily apparelling of Eliza and Georgiana and seeing them descend to the drawing-room, dressed out in thin muslin frocks and scarlet sashes, with hair elaborately ringleted.'

Some of the first full descriptions of village children just after Susan Sibbald's young days and almost contemporary with Mrs Grant's are given in a grown-ups' classic of the time which became a perennial favourite for generations and is still read. Mary Russell Mitford's *Our Village* originated in a series of rural vignettes in the *Ladies Magazine* at the end of the first quarter of the nineteenth century, published in book form from 1824 in a number of volumes spread over six years, with many new editions to follow. It includes some treasured descriptions of humble children of the time, a group so much neglected in costume chronicles of the past, in the real-life village of Three Mile Cross, south of Reading. There is the shoemaker's 'one pretty daughter, a light delicate fair-haired girl of fourteen. . . . See her on a Sunday in her simplicity and her white frock, and she might pass for an earl's daughter.' There is testimony to the continuance of the simple dress of the end of the previous century for both girls and women in the comment that getting wet 'when there is nothing in question but a white gown and a straw bonnet . . . is rather pleasant than not.' There is a further passing reference to the 'straw bonnets and cotton gowns' of country folk – which sound very like those of the fashionable. The first classless fashions had arrived, via children. The attire of the village girl from babyhood is described in one passage which constitutes a kind of complete contemporary chronicle of the six ages of girl: 'there it sits, in all the dignity of the baby, adorned in a pink-checked frock, a blue-spotted pinafore, and a little white cap. . . . One is forced to ask if it be boy or girl; for these hardy country rogues are all alike. . . . In the next stage . . . the gender remains equally uncertain. . . . It is a fine, stout, curly-pated creature of three or four – the happiest compound of noise and idleness, rags and rebellion, that ever trod the earth. Then comes a sunburnt gipsy of six . . . with . . . an old straw bonnet of ambiguous shape . . . a tattered cotton frock, once purple. . . . So the world wags till ten; then the little damsel gets admission to the charity school, and trips mincingly thither every morning, dressed in the old-fashioned blue gown, and white cap, and tippet, and bib and apron of that primitive institution, looking as demure as a Nun, and as tidy. . . . Then at twelve the little lass comes home again, uncapped, untippeted, unschooled; brown as a berry, wild as a colt, busy as a bee – working in the fields, digging in the garden, frying rashers, boiling potatoes, shelling beans, darning stockings, nursing children, feeding pigs . . . at fourteen she gets a service in a neighbouring town; and her next appearance is in the perfection of the butterfly state, fluttering, glittering, inconstant, vain . . . This is . . . the average lot of our country girls.'

Boys' clothes also are referred to several times in *Our Village*. Joe 'is a less boy than many of his companions . . . and a poorer than all, as may be conjectured from the lamentable state of that patched round frock, and the ragged condition of those unpatched shoes.' He is twelve years old, and the 'frock' was probably the traditional smock, referred to elsewhere. Jem, a boy of thirteen, bears further witness to the persistence of charity school uniforms of Tudor style. He 'is constantly arrayed in the blue cap and old-fashioned coat, the costume of the endowed school to which he belongs; where he sits all day.'

Another sidelight on boys' dress of the time is the author's description of 'my friend the little hussar – I do not know his name and call him after his cap and jacket. He is . . . about the age of eight years, the youngest piece of gravity and dignity I ever encountered . . . He stalks about with his hands in his breeches pocket, like a piece of machinery.' Again, he is 'my friend the little hussar, with his blue jacket and his immovable gravity.' The military-style dress mentioned by Rousseau as a Paris fashion had reached rural England.

The general wear of boys and men in the village is also described: 'If woman be a mutable creature, man is not. The wearers of smock-frocks, in spite of the sameness of the uniform, are almost as easily distinguished by the interested eye, as a flock of sheep by the shepherd. . . . There is very little change in them from early boyhood . . . they keep . . . the same fashions, however unfashionable; they are in nothing new-fangled.' This description is worthy of note not only in its contemporary context and as explaining Joe's 'frock' but also as the origin of a later boy's fashion, to be dealt with in due course. The wearing of dresses by small boys is also recorded in the description of Joel Brent who 'from the day that he left off petticoats, has always, in every dress and every situation . . . looked like a study for a painter.' In more detail – which again has a bearing on future boys' clothes and those of men – 'Joel is a very picturesque person, just such a one as a painter would select for the foreground of some English landscape . . . His costume is the very perfection of rustic coquetry.' He wears an open-necked shirt 'such as you commonly see in the portraits of artists, very loose trousers, and a straw hat. Sometimes in cold weather he throws over all a smock-frock.' Trousers thus appear as a traditional rural item of wear.

Infants, whose need of dress reform was greater than that of any other section of the community, unfortunately missed out on the benison of comfort and simplicity which came to all other young children from the end of the eighteenth century. Though the bad old custom of swaddling was dying out, it did not disappear for many years. This is shown by references to it by Dr William Buchan (1725–1805), whose *Domestic Medicine or the Family Physician*, first published in 1769 and the first book of its kind to appear in Britain, was a kind of Bible to mothers for many years. It was a best-seller, running into 19 large editions and about 80,000 copies in his lifetime, as well as being translated into most European languages, including Russian, and

39   The simple clothes of
ordinary children are shown in
The Hop Garden by W.F.
Witherington, R.A. (1786–1865)

becoming even more popular on the Continent and in America than in Britain. It is still being re-edited and re-issued.

Dr Buchan states that towards the end of the eighteenth century 'the practice of rolling children with so many bandages is now, in some measure, laid aside', but he also says that 'in many parts of Britain at this day, a roller, eight or ten feet in length, is applied tightly round the child's body as soon as it is born.' He disapproves strongly of this and of the general practice of encasing infants in an excessive amount of tight coverings. 'It is amazing', he says, 'how children escape suffocation, considering the manner in which they are often rolled up in flannels &c. I lately attended an infant, whom I found muffled up over head and ears in many folds of flannel, though it was the month of June. . . . Death, as might be expected, freed the infant from all its miseries.'

The roller or binder, which was a relic of swaddling bands, was often heavy and long, and it died hard, lasting until the present century in a modified form. The idea that the head should be covered at all times, indoors and out, night and day, also persisted, and often resulted in the child wearing not only a cap but also an under-cap. The latter would be close-fitting with the over-cap often frilled and lace-trimmed. Triangular pieces of lawn to be worn under the cap are frequently part of surviving layettes of the eighteenth century. Hands too were covered, and tiny mittens are found in collections of infants' wear.

In contrast to the ruthlessness of swaddling, exquisite care was given to the making of layettes. Pilches, diapers and other utilitarian coverings are not easy to trace, but are described in a number of records. The Victoria and Albert Museum collection has a tiny boned stayband, infant-size, which belongs to the eighteenth century and indicates that binders were not the only restrictions suffered by the infant. Like his elders he also wore a number of petticoats. His clothes, however, were much shorter than they were to be as the nineteenth century progressed. They were not much longer than the child itself, and dresses of fine lawn were unfussy and comfortable, very similar to those of older children. It was, however, probably better to belong to a modest rather than a fashionable family, to wear simple sprigged cottons which survive in costume collections rather than be decked out and paraded by proud mammas.

5   The End of a Golden Age

In comparison with previous fashions those introduced for children in the late eighteenth century were nearly ideal in their comfort, ease and, for the time, easy-care. Even at a period when fashions changed much more slowly than they were to do later they lasted for a long time, with only small changes.

The skeleton suit kept its character and remained the small boy's dominant fashion for nearly 50 years. From the turn of the century its trousers became somewhat wider, short jackets were more often worn and bigger boys, who had hitherto followed their fathers into breeches and full-skirted coats, also began to wear trousers, with either short jackets or cutaway tail coats. More accurately, they probably continued to wear such trousers, part of a comfortable outfit which they would be reluctant to abandon as they grew up. A similar attitude made it natural that men too should in due course adopt the childish attire – a fashion revolution in itself, and one of a kind that was to recur. But when, in 1814, the great Duke of Wellington presented himself at the fashionable Almack's wearing trousers he was refused admission. The early adult trousers, when they came to be generally worn, from about the 1830s, however, did not appear straight away as part of the utilitarian costume of the dark-suited 'city man'; they were often light-coloured and included very sophisticated 'inexpressibles', slim as tights and displaying the masculine leg for the last time in formal fashion except in Court dress.

For the early years of the nineteenth century the skeleton suit was limited to small boys. As late as 1838 Charles Dickens in *Nicholas Nickleby* describes how, when Squeers looked at Nicholas for the first time, 'he was surprised to observe the extraordinary mixture of garments which formed his dress. Although he could not have been less than 18 or 19 years old, and was tall for his age, he wore a skeleton suit, such as is usually put upon very little boys . . . Round his neck, was a battered child's frill, only half-concealed by a coarse man's neckerchief.' In *Sketches from Boz*, however, published in 1838–9, Dickens, in more fashion-conscious mood, describes 'a skeleton suit, one of those straight blue cloth cases in which small boys used to be confined before belts and tunics had come in . . . an ingenious contrivance for displaying the symmetry of a boy's figure by fastening him into a very tight jacket, with an ornamental row of buttons over each shoulder and then buttoning his trousers over it so as to give him the appearance of being hooked on just under the arm-pits.' This particular style was by then going out of fashion,

40   Boy's coat and waistcoat, early nineteenth century

41   Tom Brown, from an
illustration in the original
edition of the famous story

but Dickens himself must have worn such dress as a boy. By 1859 it was
completely out of date. In *The Haunted House*, written in that year, Dickens
describes the ghost of Master B 'put into a case of inferior pepper-and-salt
cloth, made horrible by means of shining buttons. . . . He wore a frill round
his neck'. – a relic of the past.

But from the skeleton suit emerged the long-trouser, short-jacket suit which
older boys were to wear as their normal wardrobe for much of the nineteenth
century and which in one form, the Eton suit with the very brief jacket, was
worn by younger boys at that school until the 1950s and by boys everywhere
throughout Victorian times and into the present century. In the early part of
last century, however, it was usually seen in various colour effects, such as
white or fawn trousers with red or blue jackets which developed variations.
When the historian Macaulay, (1800–59), as a youthful prodigy, was taken to
Orford to be shown to Lady Waldegrave, he wore a green coat with red collar
and cuffs, and broad, full white trousers. The coat was longer, like the later
tunic, and was described as not so pretty as the skeleton suit.

Waistcoats, single or double-breasted and in various fancy materials, were
also worn by older boys from the beginning of the nineteenth century, with
trousers and jackets; soft white shirts with frilled collars were at first fashionable for them as well as for small brothers. But by about 1820 plain linen
collars were coming in for boys of all ages. From them came the famous
Eton collar. Bows were worn at the neck by small boys, with cravats and
kerchiefs for older ones.

The top hat, first introduced in January 1797 by an enterprising London
haberdasher, caused a riot then because it frightened women and children,
but by February *The Times* wrote a leading article in support of it and it
rapidly became a fashion as keenly adopted by boys as by adults. Quite small
boys are shown wearing it in the early 1800s. The main alternative headgear
for boys was a peaked, full-crowned cap, often with a tassel, which is seen in
many fashion plates and other pictures. It seems to have some affinity with
Tudor apprentices' caps and, so far as the peak is concerned, perhaps with the
vogue for military fashions promoted by the wars of the start of the century.
White socks were usual for boys, and in addition to flat shoes, short boots
were worn, some pull-on, some laced down the sides, and, from the 1840s,
some elastic-sided.

By the 1830s restrictions were moving in around the boy's outfit. A picture
of his clothes at this time is given in *Tom Brown's Schooldays*, which describes
Tom's arrival at Rugby wearing a great coat, 'a Petersham coat with velvet
collar, made tight after the abominable fashion of those days', as the author
recalled it 20 years later, writing in 1856 of the early days of Dr Arnold's
headmastership, which lasted from 1828 to 1841. Tom arrived wearing a
cap, probably the tasselled kind favoured at the time, only to be told 'haven't
you got a hat – we never wear caps here. Only the louts wear caps.' Even his
hat, his 'go to meeting roof', was not approved, being too shiny. A new one
had to be bought at once, a 'regulation cat-skin at seven and sixpence', at
Dixon's, the approved hatter. The short jacket, the same book says, was only
acceptable for the younger boys, and its use was dictated by the wearer's
size, not age. Thus one boy's friends at home, 'having regard, I suppose, to

his age, and not to his size and place in the school, hadn't put him into tails.' As a result he was much sneered at by the bullying Flashman set. These points show something new in youthful fashions, to be transmitted later to school uniforms. It was that various features of such attire were often set by the boys, not by current trends or by those in authority. Dress taboos, likewise, were set by the young wearers.

At Tom Brown's Rugby the brilliance of the waistcoats of the older boys was also much admired by the smaller boys. There were no school uniforms. Best clothes were worn for Sundays. An incidental point is that the boys wore nightshirts but did not, like the luckier girls at Mrs Teachem's long before, have dressing gowns. When going downstairs in the mornings to fetch hot water for washing boys put on trousers over their nightshirts.

Sports clothes had not yet appeared either. When preparing for the extraordinary game of football which prevailed, with whole rival houses thronging in a body on to the field for a free-for-all, the new boy noted that 'they are hanging their jackets, and all who mean work, their hats, waistcoats, neckhandkerchiefs and braces, on the railings round the small trees . . . There is none of the colour and textures of get up, you will perceive, which lends such a life to the present game at Rugby. . . . Now each house has its own uniform of cap and jersey of some lively colour, but at the time we are speaking of, plush caps have not yet come in, or uniforms of any sort, except the Schoolhouse white trousers, which are abominably cold today.'

Small girls too continued to wear their simple, straight dresses throughout this period and the extension of this fashion first to older girls and then to women was probably partly at least due, like that of boys' trousers, to the fact that the wearers became fond of the new, easy fashions and clung to them as they grew up. The main difference in the case of girls was the further liberation of slightly shorter hemlines, which rose at first from ground to ankle-length, then gradually to mid-calf, starting with smaller girls. They then fell according to age until long skirts signified that the wearer was grown-up – a practice followed until the aftermath of World War I, which put women into knee-length dresses like those of children.

The legs were, however, strictly taboo in the early nineteenth century. It was girls who, as a result, provided a main innovation in female fashion when, about 1803, they began to wear under their shorter dresses not the time-honoured petticoats but instead trousers somewhat similar in shape to those of their small brothers, but made in fine cotton and often lace-trimmed or embroidered. These trousers were probably adopted partly to provide necessary warmth under thin muslin dresses, partly because such flimsy, blow-away skirts made some kind of modest underwear necessary for active little girls. At first the trousers were invisible, but as dresses grew shorter they came into view, remaining ankle-long. That the idea of exposing the legs was still unthinkable is shown by the fact that sometimes such 'trousers' were just cotton tubes tied on to the knees and ending at the ankles.

When, in due course, women also took to wearing filmy muslin and other types of fine cotton dresses they too wore trousers under them. Among the very fashionable and *avant garde*, led by the *merveilleuses* of Paris, tights were an intriguing alternative, flesh-coloured and regarded as very daring. They must also have had the practical advantage of being warm. Susan Sibbald's memoirs include a description of a strange British variation of the tights theme. When she was about 18, in 1801–2, and still wearing the new-style muslin dresses as her first grown-up fashions, she wore an odd kind of tights under her dresses. 'The most uncomfortable style of dress', she says 'was when they were made so scanty that it was difficult to walk in them, and to make them tighter still, invisible petticoats were worn. They were wove in the stocking loom, and were like straight waistcoats . . . but only drawn down over the legs instead of over the arms, so that when walking, you were forced to take short and mincing steps. I was not long in discarding them.' They seem to have been a kind of one-legged trouser, anticipating the famous 'hobble skirts' of a century later.

The significance of these trousers was that they introduced a new item into feminine underwear, because until this time women had not normally worn any kind of drawers or knickers. Their underwear from time immemorial had consisted of a long chemise, to which corsets or stays had been added at various periods, plus, especially in the past two or three centuries, petticoats which had varied in number and dimensions. They had been elaborated into the Elizabethan farthingale and the eighteenth-century panniers and hoops, but with none of them had drawers been worn. There is some record of drawers being worn in Italy, introduced, it is said, by Catherine de Medici, worn on occasion by courtesans, but the small girls of the early nineteenth century pioneered them into the general feminine wardrobe. Strangely, drawers were at first regarded by the older and more staid sections of the fashionable world as being both improper and unhealthy. Air, it was argued, ought to be allowed to circulate freely round the body – though how men's breeches and boys' trousers should pass this test is not explained. Also, drawers were an admission of the existence of those unmentionables – female legs.

There is an early description of Royal drawers of 1811, worn by Princess Charlotte, then 15 years old. She was talking to Lady de Clifford and it is recorded that 'she was sitting with her legs stretched out after dinner and showed her drawers which it seems she and most young women now wear.' They were still evidently something of a novelty to older women and in this case the Princess was considered too old to be showing hers – to do so was usually limited to younger girls who wore shorter dresses. The Princess, however, protested in justification 'that the Duchess of Bedford showed even more of her drawers.'

By about 1830 drawers were generally worn by women, that name being given to them when they became an item of underwear, in contrast to the girls' visible trousers or pantaloons. The adult styles for nearly a century were open in style – that is, they consisted of two separate legs, joined only by the waist-band, but those of young girls were sometimes closed at the front and sometimes also at the back, with side fastenings buttoning them up. At other times they were open at the back, or at back and front, as in an older girl's example at the Bath Museum of Costume.

The small girl of the 1830s, not in the fashionable world, had not changed

42 Trousers, later called
pantaloons, were worn by girls
with the shorter dresses of the
early 1800s. The simplicity of
the child's dress contrasts with
the elaborate one of the mother.
Ackermann plate of 1825

much in appearance, according to Charles Dickens in his picture of the ten-year-old child actress, the 'infant phenomenon' Miss Ninette Crummles, in *Nicholas Nickleby*: 'a little girl in a dirty white frock with tucks up to the knees, short trousers, sandaled shoes, white spencer, pink gauze bonnet, green veil and curl papers.' There was a moment of panic when, just before the start of her stage performance, 'one leg of the little white trousers was discovered to be longer than the other' and repairs had to be carried out with haste.

In contrast and indicative of things to come is the smart Miss Squeers in the same novel, 'arrayed in all the virgin splendour of a white frock and spencer, with a white muslin bonnet, and an imitative damask rose in full bloom on the inside thereof – her luxuriant crop of hair arranged in curls so tight that it was impossible they could come out by any accident, and her bonnet-cap trimmed with little damask roses . . . and the broad damask belt . . . which encircled her slender waist . . . and the coral bracelets which clasped her wrists.'

It is a little too elaborate, perhaps a sign that the golden age of children's fashions was beginning to pass away. That it should do so is, however, less surprising than that it lasted so long. One reason for this, and for the spread of children's fashions to grown-ups, was that in the early years of the nineteenth century Britain was cut off from France, the main source of fashion, by the French wars. No fashion lead came from Paris and, equally important, no rich French silks, satins and damasks were available to stimulate the luxury look in fashion. The English silk industry was small, but the rising cotton manufacture in Lancashire was sweeping ahead. Raw cotton imports from the East and, even more, from America, were increasing and the American civil war, which cut off that source of supply, was still far ahead.

With peace restored with France, however, simple fashions began to pall and Paris launched out into elaborate confections which soon spread to the rest of the fashion-seeking world. Fashion, being highly class-conscious, depends for its very existence on exclusivity and thereby enabling the 'top' people to be clearly distinguished from the crowd. The snobbery of fashion was henceforth to be exercised on a wider scale than ever before as the rising middle classes, swollen in wealth, ambition and pretentiousness by the industrial revolution, proclaimed their self-importance by the ostentatious dress of their womenfolk – and, increasingly, of their children. The family was a prime status symbol, demonstrating by its setting and its appearance the prosperity of the proud father who supported it. The skeleton suit and the simple white dress, for long worn by all classes, had no *cachet* left and were doomed to change. The young Victoria at the age of four, in 1823, was shown in a portrait in a large feather-trimmed hat and a fur tippet on her coat – in great contrast to her great-aunt Amelia at the same age.

'Between the years 1820 and 1825 comes the dawn of a new epoch in the history of costume', says James Laver, relating changes in the clothes of children closely to a general change. For the young it was a change for the worse. Repressive ideas, says Pearl Binder in an analysis of what happened, 'stepped on the heels of Rousseau's wild nature . . . and the children were soon the sufferers.' The clouds of glory, the idea of a pristine purity of spirit in childhood disappeared. 'Prudery', continues Pearl Binder, 'clapped pantaloons

43   Queen Victoria, aged four, in 1823, shows how fashions have moved away from simplicity

on to young girls, and boys found their necks encircled by enormous starched collars.' Corsets, tight belts and voluminous petticoats encumbered children who 'once more, with a return to piety and regular church attendance, began to be treated as imps of Satan. Victorian England fed its children on a low diet of starchy foods and skim milk to keep down their evil spirits.'

With the eclipse of the skeleton suit small boys suffered a regrettable throw-back into dresses similar to those of their sisters. Ruskin at the age of four, in 1823, wore a white dress with blue sash. At first the dresses were fairly simple, sometimes shorter than those of girls, but with the same frilly lace pantaloons showing beneath the hems and reaching to the ankles. But as time went on things got worse and small boys began to wear increasingly elaborate dresses. Fashion plates and paintings show robust little boys decked out in dresses thick with frills and furbelows, hung with lace, held out by flouncy petticoats and underpinned with frilly pantaloons. Long hair came back into fashion, and fancy hats with flowers and feathers crowned the

44 Boy's cotton suit with trousers, early nineteenth century

45 Upholstered look for the small girls of the 1830s. Yellow woollen dress with appliqué trimming, smocked bodice, pleated frills and pantaloons visible at the hem

oppressive outfits foisted on small boys by parents who themselves must have grown up in an era of happy freedom in dress. Fashion plates did not represent reality as closely as they were to do in future periods of mass production, but the dresses and the discomfort were real. When not put outright into dresses small boys fared little better in a combination of waistcoat and jacket with a pleated skirt, and with loose belted tunics worn with visible lace-trimmed drawers. Instead of the comfortable pump-style shoes of earlier days they wore tight buttoned or laced boots.

Girls and boys alike went into dresses of new, heavier materials. The muslins and cottons gave place to silks and satins and velvets, often elaborately trimmed, and the discovery of aniline dyes led to a fashion for dressing the young, like their mothers, in crimson, purple, deep blue and other strong or sombre colours. From about 1825 girls' clothes followed those of women in becoming fuller, with more elaborate shaping and various kinds of wide sleeves. Bodices were tightly fitting and tight lacing became general from early childhood, continuing right through Victorian times and becoming very rigorous for most of the period, in spite of the protests of doctors and others concerned with the health of growing children.

The upholstered look of clothing from this time coincided with a similar upholstered style of household decoration, both of them symptomatic of that pride in the solid, elaborately embellished trappings of life which was one expression of Victorian materialism and of the prosperity of at least one section of the community and of pride in the ever-growing Empire. The children, like the furniture, had to be decked out as symbols of their parents' material success and, oddly, materials like plush and velvet and trimmings like fringes and bobbles were used to embellish the coverings of both the chairs and the children. Small boys' dresses in particular were made of heavy, upholstery-type materials, differing thereby from those of girls of like age, as is seen by many examples at the Bath Museum of Costume.

Girls suffered most from the new fashions. From about 1825 their fuller skirts were braided and tucked; the fitted bodices were very tight, with rows of tucks and leg o'mutton sleeves. Pantaloons were still visible below the skirts of girls of all ages as well as of small boys. 'By 1830', says James Laver of girls' dress, 'the apex of foolishness was reached. Hats had never been so large, and probably never so uncomfortable, ranging from huge cartwheels to elaborately trimmed poke bonnets. Four or five petticoats held out the heavy velvet and woollen skirts, as they did those of women, and waists were pulled in with all the agonies of tight-lacing, imposed from early childhood by fashion-ruled mothers.'

By the mid-nineteenth century all the freedom and all the simple charm brought to children's clothes from the latter part of the previous century had been lost. 'Dress went through an unhappy period in the nineteenth century', said Margaret Jackson in *A History of Children's Dress* in 1936. 'Great pains seem to have been taken to make children look foolish and feel uncomfortable.' Similarly E. Beresford Chancellor comments: 'The childish, delightful little creatures clad in flowing, easy garments, full of the *joie de vivre*, whom we encounter in the pictures of Reynolds and Gainsborough, Hoppner and Raeburn, had turned into the rather stilted, uncomfortably dressed youngsters

46 Foolish fashions of 1840, shown in the *Petit Courier des Dames*. The girl has a full skirt and elaborate bonnet like her mother

who look out on us from a thousand canvasses which the hack portraitists of the day produced.'

Boys on the whole fared better than girls, as would be expected at the time. They emerged from their girlish dresses into a knee-length or hip-length tunic, loose and comfortable, caught in at the waist with a firm leather belt, worn at times with a white collar and paired with easy, long trousers. A link with the skeleton suit has been claimed for this innovation, which emerged in the 1830s and lasted for some 30 years, the explanation being that the shirt or tunic of the skeleton suit had come outside the trousers instead of being worn inside them. The new tunic, however, probably had more affinity with another garment borrowed from humble life, as trousers had been – the

47   Tunic worn with casual
neckerchief and country straw
hat. Master Hope Finlay by
Hill Adamson 1843–4

1   *(Detail)* Barbara Gamage, wife of Sir
Robert Sidney, later Earl of Leicester with
her children, *c.* 1600

2   The Family of Sir Richard Saltonstall by
David des Granges, *c.* 1660

countryman's smock of long tradition. It had long been worn by small boys in the country whatever their class, just as trousers had been, before becoming a fashion.

Tunics were now made in all kinds of materials, including wool and velvet as well as cotton and linen. They became general wear for boys of between four and ten in the 1840s and 1850s. Gentlemen's sons wore them as well as those of peasants, and one typical portrait of the two small sons of a prosperous Lancashire cotton manufacturer in the 1850s shows them in such tunics, apparently in black velvet, worn with Eton collars and grey bow ties, shiny black leather belts and dark grey woollen trousers of comfortable width. It was probably the most comfortable outfit of the time.

With the rise of industrialism men's clothes were becoming drab and dark by the 1830s and 1840s, when even city gentlemen were finding sombre colours a practical necessity in the atmosphere of grime and smoke which invested their factories and other work places. Boys followed their fathers in this trend, with dark suits. By the 1850s the favourite style was a dark suit

48 Practical tunics worn by boys of the 1850s. From a painting

49 Dresses, fancy pantaloons and long hair for boys in the mid-nineteenth century, as shown in *The Gazette of Fashion*

50 Collarless Zouave jackets
were widely worn by boys in
the 1850s and 1860s

with a straight, short jacket, rather like the Zouave jacket of women of the
time. The jackets were often collarless, buttoned at the neck with a single
button and sometimes edged with braid. This dismal outfit is seen in photographs of many boys of different ages in the 1850s and 1860s.

This short jacket, hitherto an unfashionable garment, worn mainly by
sailors and soldiers, first gained status when adopted for cricket by boys at
the end of the eighteenth century, either with breeches or later with the
trousers which were coming into favour for others than the small boys in
their skeleton suits. The *Sporting Magazine* in 1793 showed cricketers in white
jackets and breeches, and Dickens in 1827 described the Dingley Dellers in
'straw hats, flannel jackets and white trousers – a costume in which they
looked very much like amateur stonemasons.' By the 1850s such jackets
were being worn very generally for cricket.

From them developed, later, the blazer. It is believed by some authorities
to have been worn first in 1889 by members of one of the College Boat Clubs
at Cambridge, whose choice of scarlet is said to have given it its name. There
is also a claim that it originated in the striped jerseys worn by sailors on
H.M.S. *Blazer*, whose captain supported this derivation. However that may
be, the little boy's short jacket of the late eighteenth century became one
of the most widely worn of all garments, favoured alike by adults and young
people of both sexes and an established favourite from the 1890s until today.
Minister's Gazette of Fashion for June 1892 describes the blazer as having

'the back with no seam, front not cut away below the bottom button, Patch pockets . . . step collar . . . white, coloured, or striped flannel used.' Dark blue became popular in the early twentieth century, when the blazer became an item of everyday wear by all ages and on all informal occasions. It is perhaps the most prominent of all examples of the child being father of the man sartorially.

The female Bloomer costume of the 1850s was a spin-off from the visible pantaloons girls had been wearing for many years, but it did not have more than a brief vogue as a freak fashion. The reason given by Mrs Merrifield in her *Dress as a Fine Art*, published in 1854 and an illuminating and perceptive study of fashion attitudes of the time, is that 'Had the Bloomer costume, which has obtained so much notoriety, been introduced by a tall and graceful scion of the aristocracy, with either rank or talent, instead of being first adopted by the middle ranks, it might have met with better success . . . but it was against all precedent to admit and follow a fashion, let its merits be ever so great, that emanated from a stronghold of democracy. We are content to adopt the greatest absurdities in dress when they are brought from Paris, or recommended by a French name, but American fashions have no chance of success in aristocratic England. It is beginning at the wrong end.' She could not foresee that within a century America was to be a world leader in many fashions, pioneering mass production, 'casuals' and sports clothes and establishing a special lead in children's wear.

To the great benefit of posterity, Mrs Merrifield devotes a chapter to children's dress in her time. She looks back nostalgically to the vanished, simple clothes of the earlier part of the century. She notes that 'since the commencement of the present century, at least, children may be said to have had a costume peculiar to themselves, modified, however, by the prevailing fashion. They have had short and long waists, long and short sleeves; at one time they had trousers reaching to the heels, at another the drawers were kept out of sight, and the legs concealed in long white stockings. These again gave way to socks, and the legs were left bare to the knees.' (This refers to a brief small-boy fashion of the 1840s, to be revived in our own century).

She takes her stance firmly on a plea for the reform of children's dress, especially that of girls, and finds mid-century ideas wholly unacceptable. Describing some children at play out of doors 'on a cold and frosty evening', she notes the vast difference between the dress of the boys and girls in respect of comfort. 'The boys were all dressed in high dresses up to the throat, while the bands which encircled their waists were so loose as merely to keep the dress in its place without confining it; in short, their dress did not offer the slightest restraint on their freedom of movement. It was otherwise with the girls . . . they were dressed in low dresses, and their shoulders were so bare, that we involuntarily thought of a caterpillar casting its skin . . . when we realized that this was rendered impossible by the tightness of the clothes about the waist . . . it entirely destroyed their freedom of movement.' Because they wore tight corsets under their dresses the girls showed another difference from boys. When picking up the ball with which they were playing, 'the boys always stoop, while the girls . . . invariably drop on one knee' – they were unable to move freely because of their constricting corsets and other clothes.

Other differences also caught her attention as being equally unfair to girls. 'Whence does it arise that the boys are clad in warm dresses suited to the season, their chests and arms protected from the wintry air, and their feet encased in woollen stockings, while the girls are suffered to shiver at Christmas in muslin dresses, with bare necks and arms, and silk or thin cotton stockings?'

This leads to a general reflection on children's dress, valuable because Mrs Merrifield is one of the first writers on costume history to relate it to social conditions and human attitudes. 'Fashion', she declares from her vantage point of 1854, 'as it applies to the costume of men, is, with the exception of the hat, controlled by convenience and common sense; but with regard to the dress of women and children, neither of these considerations has any weight. . . . The dress of children, especially, appears to be exceedingly fantastic in its character and with regard to that of girls, is ill-adapted to ensure the enjoyment of health and the perfect development of the figure.' In weight, suitability to climate, evenness of covering, consideration for activity and healthy development, she finds children's clothes totally deficient. Tight-lacing is the major evil; 'so far however, from being a beauty, a small waist is an actual blemish.'

'The ignorance of mothers and nurses' and the distortions of fashion add to the troubles of girls. Boys, however, are more or less immune from the miseries imposed by fashion and human folly. She continues: 'A sensible medical writer, Dr John F. South . . . makes some very judicious observations relative to children's dress. Of the fashion of dressing boys with the tunic reaching to the throat, and trousers, which are both so loose as to offer no impediment to freedom or motion, he approves, but he condemns in the strongest terms "the unnatural" – Dr South remarks he had almost said "atrocious" – system, to which, in youth, if not in childhood, girls are subjected for the improvement of their figure and gait.'

She lays down her rules for children's dress. It should consider 'the adaptation of the costume to the climate, the movements, and healthful development of the figure; and, secondly, the general elegance of the habiliments, harmony of the colours, and their special adaptation to the age and individual characteristics of children.' All these, in her view, are neglected. She advocates light, warm clothing, flannel, even coverings for the body, allowance for activity, for freedom. But she urged in vain; many years were to pass before children were freed, and sartorially, things were to get worse before they got better.

Even infants were caught up in the elaborate and ostentatious fashions which from about the 1830s superseded the previous easy simplicity. Long clothes, which had previously usually reached only a few inches below the child's feet, became very long indeed, with skirts of more than a yard. They also became much fuller, like those of older children and of women, and they even featured fashionable puff sleeves in the 1830s and 1840s. Embroidery was used extensively to ornament them. Pelisses for out of doors were heavy and elaborate; one example in the Victoria and Albert Museum is as weighty as a woman's fur coat. Another, at Bath, in heavy cream satin, has a matching

51 Infants' dresses became longer and longer. This extreme example belonging to the early nineteenth century shows lavish embroidery

hat covered with large ostrich feathers. Under dresses and pelisses went bodices and several petticoats, and the inevitable binder, now about 4–5 inches wide and some 30 inches long, made either of flannel or of linen webbing – 'the tradition of swaddling bands was a very strong one', comment Phillis Cunnington and Anne Buck.

By the 1840s books on household and family management were becoming frequent and were widely read. Pleas for the reform of infants' clothes featured in many of them, and the follies of many current practices were pointed out in detail. An *Encyclopaedia of Domestic Economy*, by 'Thomas Webster, F.G.S., assisted by the late Mrs Parkes', which appeared in 1844, deals with the subject in some detail. 'The clothing of infants', they urge, 'should be warm, light and loose . . . that kind should be employed which may seem best adapted to secure the equal and tranquil diffusion of the blood throughout the system.' Cotton or linen had been the traditional materials for infants' underwear, but new views were now prevailing: 'flannel cannot, in this country at least, be dispensed with as an article of infants' clothing.' The length of the baby's clothes arouses sharp comment: 'Infants for the first 3 or 4 months are clothed in very long petticoats . . . they help to keep the feet of the infant safe from cold air, which would otherwise chill an infant very severely, and long clothes do also give a nurse a good hold of a child, who without sufficient clothing would be apt to slip out of her arms, but to have them so long as to trail on the ground, or to float with every move made by the nurse, so as to reach the bars of the grate, is preposterous, and even dangerous, and the good sense of every mother ought to be exerted to lay aside this worthless fashion.' Doris Langley Moore's measurements of babies' dresses of 1830 show the length to be 44 inches from shoulder to hem, and of 1870, 42 inches. Carrying was unavoidable. The first modern pram was produced in New York by Charles Burton in 1848, but was not a success, mainly because it got in the way of pedestrians. He therefore took his idea to Britain, opening a factory there with more success. The pram became fashionable when Queen Victoria ordered it for her children. The first pram in which the infant could lie down did not, however, appear until the 1870s, so infants had to be carried.

Swaddling bands are repeatedly condemned: 'the use of all bandages, swaddling clothes, tight ligatures, is most carefully to be forbidden', says the *Encyclopoedia*, implying the habit still persisted. Caps are also disapproved of. 'Caps, it is well known, are not an essential to the dress of a young infant . . . avoid caps and even more . . . heavy beaver hats, and velvet bonnets, graced with plumes and feathers, are the worst covering for a child's head that can be selected.' They harm 'the delicate tissues of the head'. To boys 'tight waistcoats and bands are very injurious' and stays for young girls are equally harmful. 'No reasonable or affectionate mother but would immediately make war with fashion rather than consign their young children to the sorrows and calamities of ill health.'

Ten years later Mrs Merrifield, in 1854, is attacking the same evils, including swaddling bands, 'which some years since prevailed universally'. She also condemns as an evil practice 'that of rolling a bandage three or four inches in width, and two or three yards in length, round the body of the child. The pain that such a bandage, from its unyielding nature, would occasion, not to speak of the ill effects on the health, can be readily imagined.'

On the subject of infants' clothing in general she is detailed and critical. 'Let us consider the dress of an infant. Here, caps, with their trimming of three or four rows of lace, and large cockades which rivalled in size the dear little round face of the child, are discontinued almost entirely within doors, though the poor child is still almost overwhelmed with cap, hat, and feathers, in its daily outings, the additional weight which the poor little neck has to sustain never once entering into the calculation of its mother and nurse.'

As regards clothing, 'the movements of the lower limbs, so essential to the healthy growth of the child, are limited and restrained, if not altogether prevented, by the great weight that we hang upon them. The long petticoats, in which every infant in this country has been for centuries doomed to pass many months of his existence, are as absurd as they are prejudicial to the child. The evil has of late years rather increased than diminished, for the clothes are not only made much longer, but much fuller. Many instances can be mentioned in which the long clothes have been made a yard and a quarter long. The absurdity of this custom becomes apparent, if we only imagine a mother or nurse of short stature carrying an infant in petticoats of this length. . . . Imagine one or the other treading on the robe, and throwing herself and the child down! We have for some years endeavoured, as far as our influence extended, to put an end to this practice, and in some cases we have so far succeeded as to induce the mother to short-coat the child before it was three months old.'

That the clothing of infants and children could harm their health but could, contrariwise, contribute to their strength and well-being was also set forth forcibly about the middle of last century by Madame Roxey A. Caplin, whose book *Health and Beauty or Woman and her Clothes* ran into several editions and attracted considerable attention. The wife of a doctor and herself a practical corset-maker with a business in Berners Street, she wrote a number of books, lectured on health and physiology, won the only medal awarded for corsetry at the 1851 Exhibition and was commended by Dr Elizabeth Blackwell, the first woman to qualify as a doctor, for 'being the first who has made the corset tolerable in the eyes of a physician.'

She condemned the then prevalent habit of 'immediately bandaging the new-born infant so heavily and with so wide an appliance that its body was severely constricted and breathing restricted.' She declared that 'all the clothes provided for the advent of the little stranger are made entirely on a false principle, and calculated to produce a baleful influence on its future development.' Chief faults were dresses that exposed neck and shoulders to the cold, tight sleeves, tied with ribbons which hampered circulation, thick napkins which restricted movement and long clothes worn for too long a time. Bonnets and head-coverings she also condemned as unnecessary. Instead, she advocated dress which allowed complete freedom – loose, even coverings that encouraged development of muscles and body.

6 Dressed-up or Drab

In spite of Mrs Merrifield's mid-century hopes that 'fashion and human folly' would no longer lay hands on boys' clothing, this was not so. Drabness, practical but not elegant, seemed to prevail for a time as boys, once freed from petticoat influence, went into dark, plain suits consisting of trousers, short jackets and sometimes waistcoats, junior versions of what men were to wear later, but some startling alternatives soon began to appear. From about the middle of the century there emerged a number of what can only be described as freak fashions for boys and others which, if not freakish, bore no relation to current fashion. 'After 1840 no rational evolution can be traced in boys' dress, which became the sport of every chaotic fancy', says Margaret Jackson despairingly of a new phase in the story of children's costume.

Quentin Bell, in his revised edition of *On Human Finery*, examines this subject and relates the elaborate dress of Victorian small boys convincingly to the theory of 'vicarious consumption' developed by Thorstein Veblen, that is, dress as a demonstration of the power and prosperity of the parents: 'The dressing of very small children gives us an example of vicarious consumption in a very pure form . . . Girls have usually worn clothes not very different from those of their mothers; boys on the other hand, being neither producers nor yet girls, had to be dressed for vicarious consumption in a new style, masculine, yet more sumptuous than that of their fathers. A great variety of styles was introduced, varying from kilts and sailor suits to lace-collared imitations of early seventeenth-century dress; there were also various school uniforms of a more or less futile character.'

There was a special degree of confusion about small boys' dress. It included skeleton suits, peg-top trousers, wide tunics, kilts. In the 1850s a new type of trousers, rather like the plus fours of the next century, were worn by boys, and even something approximating to shorts made a brief appearance about 1860, though worn with long stockings. Headgear included top hats, glengarries, and Balmoral bonnets. Various kinds of peaked caps, sometimes with the crowns as wide as tam o'shanters, also continued to be worn for much of the mid-century. Side by side with these variations and eccentricities, however, there still were plain indeterminate suits in dark woollens, with below-the-knee straight trousers and plain, often collarless jackets.

'Parents, in the unrelenting struggle for social prestige, a struggle that goes on in every home in all income groups, try to educate and dress their children

52 Freak fashions of the mid-nineteenth century included garments like the later plus-fours for small boys, as in this photograph of the 1860s, probably by Lewis Carroll

according to their own ambitions', says Pearl Binder in *The Peacock's Tail* of what was a dominant social trend in Victorian times 'The struggle', she continues, 'is usually keenest in the poorest circles, who so often dress their children above their social circumstances. . . . Kindness, comfort, convenience, count as naught beside social ambition. . . . Harshness to children, in fact, by the wearing of painful dress no less than in other ways, has been the rule rather than the exception throughout history.'

To hope and strive for the welfare and success of one's children, and indeed of all children, is bound up with all hope and belief in the value of life and the possibility of its betterment through human efforts. Such efforts, however, become meaningless and abortive unless they are based on an endeavour to understand children. It is difficult to believe that such an endeavour underlay the Victorian zeal for decking out their young in fashions which were not based on the wearers' needs or likings but on the parents' desire to establish their personal importance and wealth or their endorsement of national greatness and grandeur, past or present. They were glorifying themselves, indulging in wishful thinking, perhaps subconsciously seeking an escape from an imperfect present by building their hopes on a better future, symbolized delusively by their dressed-up children. However mixed the reasons, the Victorians showed an extraordinary zeal for dressing up their children as miniature soldiers and sailors, as Highlanders and cavaliers and almost everything except

53 Children's dress became a Victorian status symbol, with scant regard to comfort. An illustration from the widely read *Englishwoman's Domestic Magazine* of 1866

happy, care-free children. Parental tyranny, oppressions and lack of understanding of the child were all rife, behind the proud facade of triumphant
industry and triumphant imperialism.

The idea of putting small boys into versions of adult military uniforms
went far back where royalty and the nobility were concerned. There are
many paintings and descriptions of princelings attired as generals and in
various ceremonial uniforms. William, Duke of Gloucester, Queen Anne's
son (1689–1700), was at the age of seven dressed for her birthday 'in a marvellous
suit of clothes. The coat was azure blue velvet, then the colour of the mantle
of the Garter. All the buttonholes of this garment were encrusted with
diamonds and the buttons were composed of great brilliants. . . . His Majesty
presented him with a jewel of George on horseback. . . . Thus ornamented
and equipped withal in a flowing white periwig, the prince of seven summers
made his bow in his mother's circle at St James's to congratulate her on her
birthday . . . and was painted by Kneller in this outfit'; the painting is now at
Hampton Court. He died two years later, but during his little life he had his
own troop of boy soldiers whom he drilled on Wormwood Scrubs.

Napoleon was given to putting a cocked hat on the head of his infant son,
proudly called 'King of the Romans', and of buckling a sword over the white
lace frock. The small son of the Parkers of Saltram, a typical eighteenth-century
family of rank, was dressed in a complete military uniform, specially made for
him, and went to the camp of the militia with his father. There was more
practical sense in the later uniform, semi-military in style, which the Prince
Consort designed for the boys of Wellington, because he felt that the ecclesiastical style of long tunic still being worn was out of keeping with the tradition
of the college.

The spread of service-style uniforms to young people in general was,
however, a big step from these formal outfits. There was quite a vogue for
dressing small boys as soldiers about the time of Waterloo, when patriotic
fervour was high, and Miss Mitford's 'little hussar' showed that even village
life reflected that trend. There is plenty of evidence of similar fashions for small
boys. Women and girls also wore hussar jackets and other military fashions,
including epaulettes, and feathered shakos were fashionable headgear. One
small girl blazed the trail towards sex equality by appearing in full military
uniform in 1808 at the age of four! Significantly she was Amadine Lucie
Aurore Dupin, later to become famous as novelist George Sand, the most
spectacular of all pioneers of women's emancipation. At that early age, however, her attire was obviously none of her doing.

Her father, newly appointed a colonel in the Elite Guards of Napoleon, had
been transferred to the army of Italy. His wife and two daughters joined him
in Madrid in 1808 just before a week of festivities in honour of Joseph Bonaparte, created king of Spain by Napoleon. Aurore could already ride and her
mother was a clever seamstress. As described by the American Noel B. Garson
in his biography: 'she made the little girl an exact replica of the Hussar
uniform worn by Murat's cavalry honor guard. The climax of the ceremonies
in Joseph Bonaparte's honor was a mammoth military review, and when the
day arrived, Aurore rode onto the parade ground alone, with her hair cut
short, wearing her uniform and carrying a tiny sword made for the occasion

by a Spanish armorer. The little girl created a sensation. The entire crowd
applauded, Marshal Murat insisted that she ride at the head of his Hussars, and
King Joseph called a temporary halt to the proceedings while he went onto
the field himself and escorted her to a place at his side in the reviewing stand. . . .
The significance of this single traumatic experience in shaping the life of the
future George Sand was overwhelming.'

Her notorious adoption of male attire as an adult was further anticipated
when, still a small girl, she ran wild at the country estate of her grandmother
and 'sometimes, when her grandmother was taking an afternoon nap, Aurore
shed her voluminous skirts and petticoats, and donning the peasant trousers
she kept hidden at the back of a wardrobe, she practised her own tree-climbing'.
Such peasant trousers are generally regarded as the origin of boy's and men's
trousers, but Aurore added her own footnote to the story of girl's dress by
anticipating a mode of 150 years later. Finally, her masculine attire as an adult
included a long smock-like top worn with her trousers, much in the style of
young boys of the same time, the 1830s.

The first full-scale uniforms to be worn widely by boys of all ages were
variations of Highland dress. This was part of a tartan fashion which became a
positive cult. It is usually linked with the 'Balmoralomania' of Queen Victoria
and Prince Albert, part of which was an outburst of tartan furnishings all
over their beloved Highland home, bought in 1851 and rebuilt in 1853–6.
The fashion of wearing tartan, however, started much earlier than that.

54 The Prince of Wales, later
Edward VII, at the opening of
the 1851 Exhibition, when he
wore Highland dress. Detail of
a painting by Selous

55   A second generation of
Royal children remain faithful
to the kilt. The family of
Edward, Prince of Wales, in
1871, with two princes in
Highland dress

A portrait of the Prince of Wales's children in 1746 shows his son, later
George III, in a richly laced tartan coat. A small Scottish boy is among the first
recorded wearers of the kilt as we know it. The portrait of the Macdonald
boys in the Scottish National Portrait Gallery, painted in 1749–50, shows the
future Sir James Macdonald of Macdonald (1742–66) and his brother, later
Sir Alexander Macdonald (1745–95), with the older boy wearing the 'little
kilt', very much as now worn. At that time most portraits show the original
unwieldy 'great kilt', unsewn and wrapped round the body. At the time of this
painting, probably by a London-Scot, Jeremiah Davison, Highland dress
was banned by Act of Parliament, but the Macdonald boys lived in Skye,
their father was a Government supporter, so they were presumably able to
ignore the ban. Between them the boys wear 13 different kinds of tartan. The
smaller wears trews, apparently presaging the skeleton suit; both have waisted
jackets, white frills at the neck and tartan socks. The smaller holds a golf club.

Tartan was proscribed from 1746 till 1782 as a result of the Jacobite risings,
but it made a quick come-back. In 1792 Jane, Duchess of Gordon, wore a
tartan dress at the Queen's Drawing Room and then at Court, with such
success that within a few days 'tartan became the rage of all the fashionable
ladies about the town', while gentlemen went promptly into tartan waistcoats to keep up with them. In 1800 Susan Sibbald, at 17, went to the Caledo-
nian Ball, where the ladies wore tartan scarves 'over the right shoulder, and
tied with a loose knot under the left arm.' George III's appearance in full
Highland dress on his famous visit to Edinburgh in 1822, master-minded by
Sir Walter Scott, gave a new impetus to the tartan vogue, and the great fame
of Sir Walter's novels among both adults and the young had a powerful effect
on promoting the fashion throughout the land among all ages and classes.

The tartan vogue for children is also mentioned in Cecilia Ridley's life and
letters, edited by Viscountess Ridley in 1959 and recording family life in the
1840s. She describes a gown made in 1840 for eleven-year-old Alice – 'a
Douglas plaid – tight waist, tight sleeves, a most wax-like fit', made upon
'a pair of stays with bones which cause infinite trouble and dismay to the
whole household.' Another sister, Mary, also has a plaid gown. In November
1844 Cecilia writes of her own young children, Matt and Eddy: 'He and little
Eddy are both in plaid frocks and really look very nice. I did not mean Eddy
to begin, but he looked so starved by the side of his brother that I thought they
had better be alike.' The Bath Museum of Costume has versions of such frocks.

Winterhalter painted the Royal children in Highland dress in 1849 and
when, in 1851, Queen Victoria opened the Great Exhibition and was accompanied by her two eldest children, she herself described in her *Journal* for 1 May
how 'Vicky & Bertie were in our carriage. Vicky was dressed in lace over
white satin, with a small wreath of pink wild roses in her hair, & looked very
nice. Bertie was in full Highland dress.' Other members of her young family
also wore Highland dress and soon hordes of small boys everywhere were
following suit. There were also many grotesque variations of the traditional
attire. Kilt-like contraptions were worn as variations of the knee-length
tunics of small boys. White lace-trimmed pantaloons often hung below youthful kilts – but, after all, George III had worn fleshings with his kilt a generation
before.

56 Tartan sashes for party dresses became a widespread fashion, seen in a photograph of 1876

57 Young girls in plaid dresses by Julia Margaret Cameron, c.1860

The Prince of Wales appeared in Paris in Highland dress in 1855, accompanying his parents on a State visit, and created a sensation as well as spreading the fashion. America took up the tartan vogue with enthusiasm, following Britain's and Europe's lead in fashion as she had done for centuries for both adults and children. The tartans of all the clans and of no clans that ever were had a fashion bonanza across the Atlantic.

Tartan dresses for girls also became almost universal. Lady Lyttleton, who was in official charge of the Queen's children from 1842, described a children's ball at Buckingham Palace at which the two younger princesses, Helena and Louise, born in 1846 and 1848 respectively, 'looked beautiful and dear as usual, in their Highland dresses. . . . Little Prince Arthur [born in 1850] was also in Scotch dress all except the plaid.'

Royal children continued to wear Highland dress. At the wedding of the Princess Royal to Prince Frederick of Prussia in 1858, four young princes are seen in it in a painting of the ceremony. The next generation of Royal children also wore it and it remained in general favour until the 1920s brought in more relaxed fashions for the young. Scottish boys, however, remain faithful to it today. English schoolgirls wear tartan kilts, and women have adopted long kilts as evening skirts.

The sashes that went with girls' party dresses became tartan ones about the middle of last century, not always to the young wearers' satisfaction. Thackeray's daughter, later Lady Ritchie, describes how she and her sister attended a party at Charles Dickens' home wearing, with reluctance, brilliant tartan sashes, presents from one of their father's Edinburgh admirers, and austere black shoes, and being shamed by their young hostess's white satin shoes and white flounced silk dress. In Thackeray's *Our Street* (1848) Master Molyneux wears a 'flaring tartan' frock and tartan stockings with a huge feathered hat and a small dark jacket.

Not all the tartan fashions were uncomfortable or fancy-dress in style. A fashion article of the 1850s writes of 'Highland costumes which are not only prettiest for boys and girls, but also the most healthy.' Delightful and wearable silk plaid dresses for girls survive in costume collections and are seen in innumerable paintings and photographs.

From tartans to plaids was a natural evolution. That the latter were very much part of the attire of the ordinary boy is shown by that still rare thing – a detailed description of the clothing of such a one – the boy who gave his name to Charlotte M. Yonge's story *Leonard the Lion-Heart*, published in 1856. Leonard, going visiting, 'had a cap on his head, a scarlet comforter round his neck, with the ends tucked into the black belt round his sturdy waist and brown Holland blouse. His hands, with comfortable worsted gloves on, were in the pockets of his plaid trousers; but he took care that no one should see, under the blouse, that dreadful plaid tunic to match, that his mother would make him put on. If that were seen, who would ever believe that he had worn a real jacket and waistcoat every Sunday, since he was nine years old five months ago? He had been very cross because he was not allowed to wear them today to show Edwin and Aunt Jane what a man he was!' Tunic and jacket – two stages of boyhood. Edwin, in turn, is described. He is between seven and eight, but still wears real girl-clothes; a pale timid child who 'looked as if he did not like the cold air that fluttered in the long faded blue tails of his hat, which seemed made for a girl; while his short brown cloak streamed far away behind, instead of wrapping round his green frock which, as well as his short white trousers, did not give much covering to those poor little legs.' Ordinary children both of them, and neither very happy in the attire chosen for them by their elders.

By a paradox strange even in costume history, which is full of improbabilities, the most comfortable and practical of outfits to be worn by boys and also the longest-lasting and most universal, arose from the Victorian obsession with pretend uniforms – the sailor suit, and it started as a children's fashion in 1846, when Winterhalter painted a portrait of the five-year-old Prince of Wales in the sailor suit in which he had, to the great delight of the assembled crowds, appeared on board the Royal yacht, the *Victoria and Albert*, on a Royal visit to Ireland in that summer. It is a strict interpretation of naval uniform, in white with bell-bottom trousers, a top with a large sailor collar and neckerchief knotted as it should be and a wide sailor hat under which, unfortunately, fall long curls. R. Turner Wilcox, the American costume historian, says it was designed and made for the Prince by a Bond Street tailor.

It was Britain's grand boast that she ruled the seas and her navy was the proudest symbol of that rule and of her far-flung Empire. Small boys decked out as sailors brought a parental and symbolic glow of pride into every home and the Royal lead was followed with such zeal that the sailor suit became the main fashion for boys and in due course extended to girls too. It was not always as strictly naval as the Prince's and it admitted of numerous variations, though many parents were sticklers for correctness and took great pains to achieve it, with badges, insignia of rank, lanyards and whistles. A loose sailor blouse was, however, often worn with knickerbockers and later with shorts. Round cloth sailor caps with ships' names on them, and even tam o'shanters borrowed from French sailors, were alternatives to the straw sailor hat of the time. Middy suits with short page-boy jackets reminiscent of earlier boys' fashions also appeared in sailor outfits. So did peaked caps, which had also made a previous appearance as part of youthful headgear. A reefer coat was introduced about 1880. Knitted jerseys, based on those of sailors came in for children in the latter part of the nineteenth century, soon to spread to men and women and become an important part of every wardrobe from that time to today.

The sailor suit, whether for boys or girls, was also very easy to make and it was quickly drawn into the ready-to-wear market which grew apace in the children's sector after the sewing machine became a practical proposition in the early 1890s. You couldn't fault it. It satisfied parental pride. It was comfortable to wear, suited to all occasions, and it had a jolly, swaggering Jack Tar air about it which pleased the wearer as much as the parents. In the context of fashion, it had no reference to past history or present trends, but it was to have a notable influence on children's clothes of the future, to this very day.

By the 1880s sailor suits were 'almost a uniform', for boys, says Phillis Cunnington and Anne Buck. Now girls got on to the band wagon, wearing

58   The Winterhalter portrait of the five-year-old Prince of Wales in 1846 in the sailor suit which started a world-wide children's fashion still flourishing today. By gracious permission of H.M. The Queen

59   The sailor suit spread even to Russia. A 1913 Moscow photograph

60 A family group of 1870

sailor blouses similar to those of boys, with pleated skirts, usually of navy serge but also of white drill, buttoned on to under-bodices. The sailor suit had everything. It could be easy and casual for holiday and seaside wear. It could be formal if decked out with gold and silver braid. A fashion writer of the 1880s says that sailor suits are 'very elaborate' and are made for 'walking purposes, to be worn in the park and they are totally different to the regular costumes made for seaside wear.'

The fashion spread to Germany, France and other European countries. It even found its way to Russia in styles based on that country's uniforms. American mothers pounced on it, with a version similar to the uniform of the U.S. navy. Doris Langley Moore remarks that 'when a series of photographs of the Royal families of Europe was published in *The Girls' Own Paper*, there was scarcely a young prince or princess who did not appear to be going to sea.' That was at the opening of the present century, but the fashion, which had become widespread by the 1860s, was still flourishing and, like Highland dress, had been given a new stimulus by being adopted by the next generation of Royal children. There is scarcely a famous man of the period between 1880 until well into the present century who is not shown in early photographs wearing a sailor suit. A youthful portrait of Sir Winston Churchill which was treasured by his mother, Lady Randolph, shows him thus attired. Sir Osbert Sitwell's autobiography *Left Hand Right Hand*, contains a whole series of photographs of him at various early stages, but invariably sailor-suited. Every family album tells the same story, for this fashion, unlike adult ones, overrode class distinctions. It was the first time this had happened in fashion, and it anticipated by nearly a century the classless fashions of the future.

Girls took a further step towards maritime attire when they adopted, in the last two decades of the nineteenth century, a version of Scottish fisherwomen's dress. This, the last occupational dress to survive in Britain, was still being worn by the fishwives of Newhaven and Musselburgh in the East of Scotland (and still survives for special occasions). A simplified version, with navy serge turned-up tunic and red and white striped cotton skirt, was widely worn not only by Scottish but also by English schoolgirls. It lasted for more than a generation, and was still being worn to some extent in the years up to the First World War.

The American influence on children's clothes, which was to become dominant in the twentieth century, began about the 1860s. Unlike the earlier Bloomer fashion for women, it was successful, though a reversal of the long tradition by which Americans had followed European fashions and even sent to Europe for clothes. George Washington, for instance, had dispatched an order to London in 1759 for clothes for his step-daughter, Miss Custis, including pack thread stays, a stiffened coat, gloves and masks (a protection against sunburn) and in 1761 he sent a larger order for clothes for both his step-children, including sophisticated coats and dresses and white kid gloves.

The first reversal of this custom made its big impact among British boys in the 1860s, though its origin lay in the early years of the century. Knicker-bockers, which boys began to wear as an alternative to trousers, were a sensible innovation. They acquired their name from the *nom de plume* under which Washington Irving in 1848 wrote his burlesque *History of the World*. When this was illustrated in 1859 by George Cruikshank, the English artist dressed the old Dutch settlers in the full breeches of the seventeenth century, when New York was New Amsterdam. This led to the garments being introduced as sports or country wear for men and as a new and highly popular variation for the boy's wardrobe, with the American name. Originally they were loose breeches gathered at the knee, but the styles for boys varied and by 1870 they included a straight open-ended version, reaching to below the knee at first and worn with stockings. By the end of the century they rose above the knee, producing the first version of that symbol of boyish freedom – shorts.

In our era of casual clothes shorts have become a universal garment, worn by both sexes and all ages for sport and on the beach, as well as by some small boys for general wear. They thus became another fashion started by children and passed on to the rest of the community.

By the 1870s various kinds of knickerbockers and chopped-off trousers were being worn by boys along with another sensible innovation: the Norfolk jacket, with box pleats down the sides and a slotted waist belt. It has been explained as derived from the boy's tunic, which to some extent it replaced. It was usually worn with a white Eton collar and was made in thick dark wool. Men also wore it as a sporting outfit, originated by the then Duke of Norfolk, but whether the youthful or the adult version came first is doubtful. The boy's was, however, much more widely worn.

61 Variations on the knicker-bocker suit included chopped-off trousers and various jackets, including Norfolk and sailor styles, in dark wool

That the sailor suit brought freedom and comfort to its wearers was accidental and unconnected with its origins in a fantasy attitude to children's dress. Evidence of this lies in the fact that the 1880s, which saw the sailor suit in its heyday, also witnessed the introduction of the ultimate in unrealistic costume for boys, the Fauntleroy suit.

Cavaliers, Spanish grandees and historic courtiers had already had small counterparts in Victorian boys whose velvet party suits, lavishly lace-trimmed, are recorded from the mid-nineteenth century. Such outfits did not, however, enter the mainstream of youthful fashions until the advent of the Fauntleroy suit. This owed its name and fame to the story *Little Lord Fauntleroy* by Anglo-American novelist Frances Hodgson Burnett, which was serialized in America in 1885 and published in book form in 1886. It is usually regarded as the first American fashion to capture the British scene, but it appeared in England before that date. In 1884 the *Tailor and Cutter* described the suit as party dress or 'fancy dress', one of many worn by small boys in the evening. It was also illustrated in *The Lady* in 1885, before the serial had started, and was described in all its glory as intended for 'a little fellow of seven . . . tunic and knicker-bockers of sapphire blue velvet and sash of pale pink. Vandyke collar and cuffs, if not of old point lace, should be of Irish guipure.' The hero of Mrs Burnett's book was subdued compared with this, wearing a black velvet suit with a red or black sash, though he did have a plumed Cavalier hat over his curls, as shown in Reginald Birch's famous illustrations.

In America, as in England, the Fauntleroy suit was part of a fancy dress tradition evident in children's clothes since the 1830s, according to R. Turner Wilcox, who cites the Scottish kilt and the sailor suit as examples of the same trend. The Fauntleroy suit, however, went to extremes in that it paid such scant attention to the wishes of the wearers and was, as much as any of the miniature grown-up clothes of bygone children, dictated by adult vanity. Mothers loved it and women's magazines continually praised it to the skies: 'Nothing can be better than the Charles the First dress, generally made in dark velveteen or satin. The tight knickerbockers have sashes', says one of them. Another praises 'huge square collars made of the finest silk cambric enhanced by a wide row of delicate lace such as imitation point.'

The history of the Little Lord Fauntleroy suit is well summarized by Ann Thwaite in her recent biography of the author, *Waiting for the Party*. The original of the character was Frances's elder son, Vivian and, according to later records, the family 'knew how much Vivian had suffered all his life from his identification with Little Lord Fauntleroy.' Frances had 'a weakness for picturesque clothing' and 'the boys had blue jersey suits with red sashes and they also had best suits of black velvet with lace collars.' Such suits 'were by no means unusual wear for small boys at this period', says Miss Thwaite, 'a year or so before the Fauntleroy suit spread their appeal.' Frances herself stated that the character was based on Vivian, 'just Vivian with his curls and his eyes, and his friendly, kind little soul.' The illustrations were based on an 1884 photograph of Vivian.·

Once the book was published in October 1886 it became an immediate success, rose to be one of the biggest best-sellers of all time and sold over a million copies in England alone. It was translated into more than a dozen languages, and earned Frances at least $100,000 in her lifetime. It was produced as a play in New York and in London in 1888. It was repeatedly filmed, with Buster Keaton playing the name part when he was 10 and Freddie Bartholomew appearing in another version in 1916. In 1921 Mary Pickford,

62   One of the original illustrations of *Little Lord Fauntleroy*

at 27, doubled as the little Lord and his mother, 'Dearest', a name actually used by the boys for Frances. Mary visualized her Little Lord Fauntleroy as the peak of her film career and it had an immense success. Attending the première of this film was, incidentally, Frances's last public appearance, three years before her death in 1924. A new version of the film was announced in 1976, as was a T.V. serial.

In the face of publicity unequalled in any area of fashion before or since, there was no stopping the cult of Little Lord Fauntleroy. It was a mania in Britain and America. Usually against their will, small boys were forced into it everywhere, often with the further indignity of curls. Compton Mackenzie recalled how in 1889, when he was six, he suffered from 'that confounded Little Lord Fauntleroy craze which led to my being given as a party dress the Little Lord Fauntleroy costume of black velvet and Vandyke collar. . . . The other boys at the dancing class were all in white tops' – to sailor suits, more formal than blue tops. The indignity was, however, dealt with forcibly: 'Naturally the other boys were inclined to giggle at my black velvet, and after protesting in vain against being made to wear it I decided to make it unwearable by flinging myself down in the gutter on the way to the dancing-class and cutting the breeches, and incidentally severely grazing my own knees. I also managed to tear the Vandyke collar. Thus not only did I avoid the dancing class, but I also avoided being photographed in that infernal get-up.' Sir Adrian Boult recorded that the fashion was still raging in his youth, 'about 1894 or '95'. The long hair fashion also persisted. Elizabeth Haldane wrote of her son Jack, born in 1890 and later to become famous as Professor J.B.S. Haldane, that 'Jack was a beautiful child. In those days it was not done to cut small boys' hair short, so I kept his long lint-white locks until he went to school.'

Probably no fashion has ever been so hated by the wearers as the Fauntleroy suit. Vivian detested it as much as anyone, and was a normal boy, tough on occasion, who disliked dressing up. But the suit pursued him. As late as 1914, when Frances arrived in New York from London visits, the *New York Telegraph* ran a banner headline: 'Lord Fauntleroy greets mother'. Reginald Birch said at the end of his life that the Fauntleroy drawings had ruined his career.

The drawings were probably the main cause of the trouble – and the fashion. In fairness to Mrs Burnett and her Cedric it should be stated that the descriptions of his appearance are few and brief. Before the discovery of the title he walked out 'with his nurse, wearing a short white kilt skirt, and a big white hat set back on his curly yellow hair.' The first suit that was to be given his name was not at all grand. In Fifth Avenue 'ivvery man, woman and choild lookin' afthre him in his bit of a black velvet skirt made out of the mistress's ould gownd' was admiring an outfit made by Mary, the servant and general factotum. In the whole book there are only some six brief descriptions of the boy's clothes, all incidental apart from the classic one of his arrival at the stately home he was to inherit: 'What the Earl saw was a graceful childish figure in a black velvet suit with a lace collar, and with lovelocks waving about his handsome, manly little face.'

7 Changing Fashions for Victorian Girls

Girls' fashions of the mid-nineteenth century did not descend to the drabness of some of those worn by boys, nor did they compete with the quasi-historical fantasies of the Fauntleroy cult.

The only independent contribution made by girls to the fancy dress or fantasy fashions for the young in Victorian times was the red, hooded party cape. It was almost a party uniform for small girls until the second decade of this century and there are references to it and pictures of it being worn in Victorian books and magazines. How far back it went is difficult to estimate, but there seems no doubt that its origin lay not in the fashion world but in the fairy tale Red Riding Hood. Iona and Peter Opie, authorities on the history of the fairy tale, see this as the likely source of the child's red cloak. Looking further into the subject, Iona Opie recalls: 'Red flannel seems to have been the usual material for warm woollen petticoats and cloaks. Probably it was cheap, and wore well. I think,' she continues, 'that in the era of the party wrap the idea of a red-hooded cloak was probably associated with Red Riding Hood in people's minds.' The flannel became serge or some other warm wool for the party version, but the style remained unchanged through the years.

The Opies record the history of this, one of the most loved of all fairy tales, in *The Classic Fairy Tales*. It first appeared in Perrault's 1695 book of fairy tales, published in France. They say that, 'the red "chaperon" was, as far as we know, one of the details Perrault added when he retold the traditional story, but that kind of hood was standard wear in his day, so one cannot say he invented it.' The word was translated as 'riding hood' in the English edition of Perrault, *Histories or Tales of Past Times*, which appeared in 1729.

The story was a favourite of eighteenth-century children and was included in anthologies. The cape was shown in 1771 and was one of the first illustrations by Thomas Bewick, born in 1753. There was a Red Riding Hood pantomime in 1803, say the Opies, and the red hood was seen in 1804 in a hand-coloured engraving in Tabart's *Popular Stories for the Nursery*, the first collection of such tales to have coloured illustrations. Dickens said the story of Red Riding Hood was his first love. The cape was probably worn through most of the nineteenth century – and in the present one until the modern child of the 1920s turned away with scorn from such whimsical nostalgia.

In general, however, girls followed with distressing closeness the extra-

63 Children's fashions for 1871 had nothing childlike about them. *Englishwoman's Domestic Magazine*

vagances of women's fashions and lost the charming simplicity introduced in the 1770s and retained for nearly half a century. Skirts now became fuller, and under them petticoats became equally full and more and more numerous. Waists were tighter, and that meant the wearing of stays laced to extremes from an early age. Materials for dresses became heavy and their colours strong or sombre. Fashion for girls, says Marion Lochhead of the 1850s, 'bolted into extravagances of a most unattractive sort.' Even tiny girls wore dark velvets, glacé silks, feathered hats, dresses trimmed with passementerie, black velvet ribbon and braid. Girls followed their mothers into crinolines to some degree and references to youthful crinolines occur in *The Englishwoman's Domestic Magazine* and in girls' stories of the time, including those of Juliana Horatia Ewing. Schoolgirls in crinolines appear in the best-selling novel *Comin' Through the Rye*, by Helen Mathers, which deals with the 1870s. The narrator, when aged 12 or 13, laments: 'How my gowns, petticoats, crinolines, ribbons, ties, cloaks, hats, bonnets, gloves, capes, hooks, eyes, buttons, and the hundred and one etceteras that make up a girl's costume, chafe and irritate me.' In more detail she describes the crinoline in an account of her 16-year-old sister, Alice, being involved in a 'crinoline row' with her tyrannical Victorian father: 'Alice loves a big crinoline . . . papa hates it; and as sure as ever her petticoats swell beyond a certain limit, there is a fearful to-do. . . . Now Alice knows the length of tether permitted to her perfectly well . . . but . . . she has forgotten her parent's little prejudices, and stands before him confessed in all her amplitude of five yards and a half.' The crinoline expands and contracts according to father's temper: 'If he is in an amiable or engrossed mood, she usually lets out an extra reef or two; if he is in a bad one, she collapses at a moment's notice, and looks like a folded butterfly.' Now he threatens to burn it.

That, and the photographic illustrations, show the veritable metal cage of

64 Real-life crinoline in a
photograph of a girl of 1865.
Pantaloons are still worn

65   Dark velvet coat, silk-
trimmed, for a four-year-old
of 1876

the crinoline worn by both girls. In some ways the crinoline was a relief from
the oppressive petticoats. When in the 1870s, it was followed by back-drawn
draperies and the *tournure*, or bustle, girls' dresses again followed the adult
line, which was tight, cramping and devoid of youthfulness, down to the
elaborate tight, buttoned boots or the even more elaborate ones made of
satin and laced up over open fronts.

That is the picture conveyed by the fashion plates, the fashion magazines and
the photographs of girls dressed in their best for the occasion. But a more
cheerful and probably a more true-to-life picture emerges from the immortal,
Alice in Wonderland, published in 1865 with its equally immortal illustrations
by Sir John Tenniel. Alice is a spirited, uninhibited, outspoken little girl,
though always a polite one, and her clothes too are unrestricting. She seems
to presage the New Woman who was to create a stir a generation later; to
suggest a future candidate for the Girton College which was to be founded
four years later in the Cambridge of Lewis Carroll, elderly bachelor, parson

3   The Graham Children by Hogarth
(1697–1764)

4 A fashion plate of 1831

and mathematical don – the most unlikely of creators of the most loved and most famous little girl in literature.

Alice's clothes were based on those worn at the time of the book and, like Little Lord Fauntleroy's outfit, preceded the book. They go, however, to the other extreme from his and foreshadow the more practical future instead of echoing the romantic past. In her normal attire Alice has none of the velvets and furs, trimmings and frills, ribbons and flowers, laced-up boots and prim gloves of fashion-plate girls of her time. She wears a simple dress with a plain bodice and a straight, full skirt with some rows of tucks at the hem, to allow for her growth. The dress has short puff sleeves and a tiny turn-down collar. Over it goes a pinafore, also with small sleeves, plus two pockets. Her hair is simply brushed back, uncurled, and she has plain, light stockings and flat ankle-strap shoes with rather square toes. Her clothes do not stop her from swimming vigorously in the pool of her tears. She falls down holes without becoming entangled in her skirts and petticoats and she runs at top speed to fetch the white rabbit's fan and gloves.

66 Alice in Wonderland, as drawn by Sir John Tenniel

Six years later, when *Through the Looking Glass* was published, Alice has changed considerably in appearance, but keeps her freedom of dress. The actual dress itself is similar, but the apron is frilled and tied with a large bow at the back, whereas previously it was simply buttoned at the waist. Her hair is now caught back with what has become generally known ever since as the Alice band. Another change is that she now wears wide striped stockings. These were a new development in the wear of both boys and girls from the 1850s, a large selection of them being shown at the Great Exhibition of 1851 and still preserved in the Bethnal Green Museum of Childhood. They are seen in endless photographs of young people from that time. They are a surprising development in girls' wear, because they draw attention to those previously concealed or disguised legs. But red and white and blue and white horizontally striped stockings were very popular in the 1860s and 1870s, when scarlet stockings were also widely worn. Bright stockings disappeared in the 1880s, when black, brown and grey became usual. But identical striped stockings, and tights, reappeared on the fashion scene in 1976, for girls and women.

67 Alice as the complete fashion-plate little girl when she turns into a Queen in *Through the Looking Glass*. Also by Tenniel

When Alice finds herself in a train she wears the current formal fashion for little girls and is shown by Tenniel wearing a neat, fitted jacket, a pork-pie hat with a feather standing up stiffly in front, a barrel muff and trim little dark boots over the striped stockings. She even has a small handbag on the seat beside her. When, at the end of the story, she turns into a queen, she appears in an elaborate fashionable dress, with a double skirt formed by a frilled polonaise caught up in a bustle over a flounced under-skirt, little light-coloured boots, rows of large beads, plus a formal crown. She is the complete fashion-plate little girl.

Under her sensible dress Alice would wear the usual garments of the time – chemise, stays (presumably not too constricting), drawers, perhaps of the closed, side-fastening kind derived from pantaloons, which had become shorter and invisible a few years previously. Her stockings would be kept up by garters as suspenders did not come into existence until the late 1870s, first as a kind of separate harness and later as a belt worn over the corset. Not

till 1901 did they become part of that garment. Alice's petticoats were probably two white and one flannel, but the latter does not seem to have been of
red flannel. It could have been, because the red flannel charisma extended to
the child's wardrobe as well as to that of the adult woman.

What was the reason for it? What magic was there in red? Louisa Kathleen
Haldane, who was born in 1863, asked but could not answer that question in
her memoirs *Friends and Kindred*, published nearly a century later: 'What, I
wonder, was the fetish connected with red flannel? If old Mrs Somebody at
the lodge was rheumatic, quite the best present to give her would be a red
flannel petticoat, or possibly a bed-jacket, only be sure it was red flannel.
As for my personal wear, my nightgowns were red flannel, and there was a
sudden change when I was about nine years old and they became white
cotton.' Some five years later she chose material for her first shop-made
dress and jacket – and the jacket had to be lined with red flannel, though this
was by then unusual and made her different from other girls. The red-flannel
nightgowns, incidentally, were not recklessly discarded. A use was found for
them in that prudent Scottish household. At Cannes 'that summer sea-bathing
was prescribed for me. My red flannel nightdresses were made into bathing
dresses (grown-ups wore bathing dresses made of thick blue serge with
patterns of white or red braid).'

Other points about girls' fashions of the time are made in her book. An
1865 picture shows her as a two year old in a dark dress with full skirt, white
socks and little boots, with drawers still showing. At six she wears a dark
velvet dress and an Alice band. On clothes generally, she says: 'I seem to recall
that one's clothes were almost always of very thick or very thin material.'
Summer clothes could not for any reason be worn before 1 May, then they
were adopted whatever the weather. A curious point, confirmed by many
photographs, is: 'What strikes me as really queer is that after I ceased to wear
childish straight frocks with a large sash, we – my contemporaries and the
older generation – scarcely ever had a dress made entirely of one material.
We did not just trim our cashmere or merino with silk or poplin; we inserted
panels of a different material if not of a contrasting colour.' In 1877 she wore
a boater, with a bunch of buttercups on front of the brim. In 1879 no flowers
were the fashion – but, she notes, 'in 1956 boaters were back again, with
flowers as before!' Very exclusive 1976 schoolgirls went back to boaters with
ribbon bands in school colours.

What was to be called the women's movement, already stirring in the mid-
nineteenth century, did not have any immediate liberating effect on fashion,
either adult or juvenile. On the contrary, it intensified the discomfort and
pretentiousness and general elaboration of what was worn. The leaders of the
emancipation movement were not, with rare exceptions, drawn from the
high society which set fashion. The rising middle classes followed that society
and, for the most part, they were anxious to see the *status quo* retained; to rise
upon the rungs of a stable society and not to undermine it. They were also
enjoying a more busy and varied life in the leisured and monied state which
invested the middle- and upper-class woman. In this life, centred largely
round the family, children played a greater part than before, accompanying

their mothers on visits and other activities of the busy social round. Their smart and fashionable appearance was part of the image of social success or aspiration to be presented to the world; they were therefore much dolled up. Girls and small boys suffered most, older boys escaping into school uniforms and school life. It is a symptom of the times that from the mid-century children appear with their mothers to an increasing extent in the fashion plates which played a much more important part in the dress world than today because ready-to-wear clothing barely existed in the context of fashion. Fashion plates and paper patterns were the main means of communicating fashion.

The clothes worn by normal middle-class children in the 1870s are described by Eleanor Sillar in her book of reminiscences, *Edinburgh's Child*. Born in 1869, she describes early childhood walks with Ann, her nurse, and her brother Louis. She recalls how 'I thought Louis adorable in his dark blue coat and scarlet stockings, with the glengarry bonnet on his long yellow curls.

68   The mixing of different materials added to the fussiness of girls' fashions in the 1880s. Here in 1882, plain and patterned, plus frills and white lace collars and cuffs for two sisters dressed identically

69   All dressed up in 1880. Note
the boy's frilly knickers

How I hated my own coat of black persian lamb cloth.' Starting school at a 'Private Establishment', she describes 'two timid babes, blue-eyed, with long yellow curls, Louis in a belted tunic, me in a short frilled frock.'

An evening event, she continues, is 'a clean pinafore, and dessert in the dining room', but for a grown-up party she is allowed to attend 'I have on my new velvet frock. "Real velvet," says Ann with awe and I know that it has cost six pounds and that I am considered a most fortunate little girl to possess such a frock.' Dressed up for Sunday, she describes her appearance. 'My curls like glossy sausages, hateful to me, are her [Ann's] peculiar pride and care; my black button boots shine; not a wrinkle shows in my ribbed white cotton stockings. Perhaps I have on my new frock, pale grey with little pleats. I am very proud of it, for it has been made for me at MacLaren's in the High Street instead of by Ann's niece . . . My hat is a pale lemon-coloured straw, scuttle-shaped, and the palest of pale blue neckties is tied under my chin. But alas for vanity! "It is all too colourless", said my father impatiently. . . . Dashed but undaunted, Ann rose to the occasion. She flew, and fetched my coral necklace . . . she added a silver chain below the necklace, then capped the colour scheme with a second coral necklace.'

Children's fashions changed continually. To start with 'in my nursery days frocks for little girls were apt to be modelled on grown-up styles', and a photograph of her at eight shows her in what she describes as a vivid purple dress with shaped bodice. There followed 'Sunday frocks, party frocks, school frocks, from the days of starchy white piqué with frills and a Roman sash, and a hideous garment called a "polonaise", from my lilac poplin with black velvet bands stitched across my front like the bars of a grate, on to the time of the prettier Princess fashion.' They all sound unchildlike, at least up to the Princess one.

The general discomfort of young people's clothing in the 1870s is also recalled by another Haldane, Elizabeth, born in 1862 and author of *From One Century to Another*, written long afterwards. She says that 'the overclad babies, with their often lovely embroidered frocks above the multitude of string-confined undergarments, probably suffered most', but finds little joy in the dress of children in general. 'Thick woollen stockings, tied up with garters, were worn by both boys and girls, and the girls had, in addition, to wear many petticoats of flannel and even of eiderdown in winter. Everyone who suffered in those days recollects the clothing that tightly compressed the neck, the frills, the "comforters" that were no comfort. . . . Both sexes wore stays, though boys discarded them about the age of seven, while the girls were sentenced for life, as each year they became stronger and more bony.' The pram had not reached the nursery in her childhood. 'Our nurse', she says, 'always carried the babies in her own arms; she would have disdained a perambulator or any mechanical aid.' Progress had still a long way to go.

8 Clothes Reforms Return

In spite of much sensible and enlightened writing by Victorians on the need for freedom in children's dress, up to about 1880 it did not seem that the efforts of the past 40 years had borne much practical fruit, except for the remarkable lucky accident of the sailor suit which, adopted as part of fancy dress, proved the greatest step forward ever taken towards youthful dress reform. Apart from that, the simplicity of the start of the century now looked like a false dawn and young people, especially girls, were reverting to being miniature adults in a period of fashion as irrational and uncomfortable as anything in the past.

But rescue was at hand. Fashion's orbit was widening with the rise of the middle classes who, though class consciousness made many of them follow the mode in its extravagances, also included a strong intellectual element devoted to social reform. The whole basis of society was being questioned and in the years between the 1830s and the 1880s great steps had been taken to remedy numerous glaring wrongs, including the horrors of child labour and the plight of orphaned and abandoned children. That did not in itself improve the character of children's clothes, but as part of a growing recognition of children's rights and of their special needs it had a wider, more practical and more lasting effect than that exerted by the more idealistic and poetic enlightenment of the eighteenth century. As clothes reform became part of social reform, children's requirements in this respect were given recognition and considered on their own merits.

Such clothes reform needed to be given more impetus than could be achieved by the written words of fashion experts, however dedicated, and the impetus came from several directions almost simultaneously and sometimes fortuitously in the 1880s. Dr Gustav Jaeger's Sanitary Woollen System, applying health principles to clothing with German thoroughness, was a revolution in attitudes to the subject. In a long leader page article *The Times* called it 'a new gospel' soon after Mr L.R.S. Tomalin, in 1884, brought the system to Britain, when he not only translated and published Dr Jaeger's book, *Health Culture*, but also acquired British rights in the Jaeger name, publications and system and, to complete the circle, started manufacturing and selling Jaeger clothing. *The Lancet* and the *British Medical Journal* both voiced strong approval of the health-giving properties of wool, and the cult immediately became fashionable, attracting devotees as diverse as Oscar

70 The idea of wool for infants was long-lasting. This all-wool 57-piece layette was presented to H.M. The Queen in 1960 by 16 spinner members of the Hand Knitting Wool Council for the infant Prince Edward

Wilde and Bernard Shaw. Children, now a cause for concern among reformers, were among the first to benefit from the new vogue and for generations to come 'wool next to the skin' was an inflexible rule for every self-respecting mother of infants and children of all ages. Mrs Douglas in her much-read *The Gentlewoman's Book of Dress* (1890?) says: 'In keeping a baby warm the great thing is to begin next the skin, and have one or two woollen garments first of all . . . Jaeger makes the daintiest little woollen shirts for babies in the finest and softest of wool . . . A cream-coloured woollen dress is more artistic, just as pretty, and a great deal warmer than that of linen or cotton. It is indubitably better in winter for a baby.' It was a revolution at the time; the application of scientific knowledge to dress, as made by Dr Jaeger, had never previously been developed.

Almost simultaneous with Dr Jaeger were other approaches to dress reform through the creation of new fabrics. Working with two prominent doctors, Mr Lewis Haslam, MP for Newport, Monmouthshire, produced a cotton-based cellular material based on the same general principle of porousness which underlay Dr Jaeger's system. This was Aertex, devised to admit air and thereby insulate the body against heat and cold. A company to manufacture it was set up in 1888 and it was soon adopted for children's underwear and outerwear, for which it became – and remained – very popular, Viyella, a blend of cotton and wool which also proved very suitable for children's wear, came into production in 1891, and also became a speciality for young people's clothes.

71   No signs of reform in the
1870s. A dress of ribbed blue
silk and velvet with boat neck
and short sleeves is completely
impractical. It was fashions of
this kind that Mrs Ballin decried

Closely linked in purpose with Dr Jaeger's theories of health through clothes
was the Rational Dress Society, founded in 1881 and vigorously living up to
its name under its president, Viscountess Harberton. Young people as well
as adults were the target of the reformed dress advocated and demonstrated
at crowded meetings and at two exhibitions, the first in 1883, the second and
more important the International Health Exhibition of 1884. The first and
most notable contemporary account of how the Society was affecting
children's dress and how the subject was regarded by the reformers is recorded
in a lecture by Ada S. Ballin given at the exhibition on 14 July 1884 and
published in the same year by the exhibition's executive council and the council
of the Society of Arts.

Mrs Ballin, an established writer on dress and editor of the late nineteenth-
century magazine *Baby*, took a new look at her subject. 'Dress', she stated,
'should be looked upon from a scientific point of view. It is in truth one of the
great powers which preserve or destroy health and its influence is increasingly
felt from birth to death.' She has much to say about the need to protect children
from cold: 'What father . . . would think it salutary to go about with bare
legs, bare arms, and bare neck? Yet this is exactly what most people allow
their children to do.' She inveighed against heavy and restrictive clothing with
equal fervour and added her condemnation to that made for more than a
century of 'the binder or swather', surely the most persistent of all misguided
items of infant attire. She quoted an attack made in the previous year by
Prof. Humphrys at the Congress of the Sanitary Institute of Great Britain
on how 'those mischievous two yards of calico . . . constrict and hinder the
expansion of that very region of the body where heart and lungs, stomach
and liver . . . are struggling for room to grow and do their work . . . A more
pernicious device can hardly be conceived than this relic of ancient nursedom.'

She finds baby clothes in general 'made according to a bad old fashion',
too low in the neck, too tight at the arms, impossible to put on without
turning the child over, too long, too full and too heavy. She disapproves of
waterproof drawers and insists that *infants do not need caps indoors* – the italics
are hers and so it evidently was a sore subject, despite earlier writers' efforts.
She approves 'a little spencer' which sounds like the still familiar matinée
coat, and woollen vests, which seem to be a novelty: 'I have seen some very
nice vests for infants knitted of fine wool', which, she explains, stretch and cling.

Of older children she says: 'Boys and girls should be dressed alike until the
boys are breeched', thus indicating the persistence of dresses for boys. She also
lays stress on the need for separate types of clothing for young people as
opposed to adults, including girls' drawers and petticoats, the latter fastened
to a bodice. Also, she continues, 'combination drawers and vest are very
convenient and good.' They had been introduced by Dr Jaeger. Any gaps
between items of children's dress distress her deeply; she does not seem to
take account of summer heat. Thus 'socks ought never to be worn, and the
stockings should be pulled up about a couple of inches above the knee of the
drawers which ought to fit round the knee and be fastened with suspenders
to the bodice under the petticoats, as the pressure of garters is injurious.'
Suspenders were then very new, having first been introduced in 1878, but
garters continued to be worn until well into the present century.

Crocheted or knitted winter dresses of thick Berlin wool are also recommended for the young child, and should 'like all children's dresses, be made to reach throat, wrists, and ankles, not according to the absurd fashion of making dresses low where they ought to be high, and high where they ought to be low.' But materials should be light, strong and durable, 'so that the child may not suffer from being forbidden healthy play, lest its clothes should be spoiled.'

Of white she strongly approves; it should always, in her view, be worn next the skin. White dresses, advocated for both summer and winter, have the advantage that they show dirt and are therefore hygienic. Aniline dyes, which as already said, were making strong coloured clothes fashionable for children at this time, are declared to be a poison. Red flannel is particularly injurious because salts of tin are used in the dye. So much for the time honoured protector against cold! Parents who dress up their children for their own glorification are also condemned by Ada Ballin: 'If a woman wants a block to set fine clothes on, let her get one made of wood or wax, and not turn her little boy or girl into one.'

For boys, who 'should be breeched as soon as they begin to run easily, Jersey suits are most healthy and comfortable, and may be worn until the child is six or seven'. Revolutionary is her suggestion of similar outfits of this kind for girls as well as boys: 'It is a pity that little girls as well as boys should not enjoy the freedom of Jersey-knicker-bocker and sailor suits, but prejudice is against this at present . . . About the best dress I know of for girls from three years upwards is Miss Frank's kindergarten frock, which consists of a sort of smock over a divided skirt' which would 'greatly benefit girls' health if generally adopted and would prevent them when grown up wearing unhealthy fashionable dress.'

Of two dominant children's fashions of her day Ada Ballin took opposite views. Highland dress she regarded with horror: 'Scotch suits for boys which are so fashionable, and so much admired, are an abomination owing to the way in which they expose the legs.' She quotes the case of a boy of six who had not grown since he was three because his legs were thus exposed! But sailor suits win her full approval: 'A very pretty and nice dress for boys when breeched is the sailor's suit which, by its looseness, allows free movement, is

72 Real-life boys' clothes of the 1880s owed little to the reformers but were varied and practical. An 1883 outfitter's advertisement

very durable and covers all the limbs.' She recommends it for all and 'it may be worn until the boy is old enough to wear ordinary trouser suits.'

The Aesthetic Movement in dress of the 1870s and 1880s, with its 'greenery, yallery' cult and its folksy trends, is usually regarded, like the Rational Dress Movement, as a failure in that it attracted only a minority to its loose, flowing styles and did not achieve its basic purpose of drawing in the masses and proving a social force. But it had a strong and lasting influence on the dress of children, especially girls, and did much to foster a separate category of comfortable attire for them which was finally to be established in the early twentieth century. One of the first records of this is the small girl seen in Frith's famous documentary painting *Private View at the Academy* (1881), in which the child and her mother both wear the new aesthetic dress. Six years later Frith described the picture in his memoirs, saying that 'on the left of the composition is a family of pure aesthetics, absorbed in affected study of the pictures' – and incidentally talking to Robert Browning. The girl's dress has a full bodice, its loose folds continuing down the skirt below the waist belt. It has full sleeves and, though mid-calf in length, is otherwise the complete opposite of contemporary fashions, also shown in the picture, with their close-fitting bodices, tight back-drawn skirts and draped bustle effects.

Ada Ballin in her *Science of Dress in Theory and Practice* (1885), also showed how much attitudes to the young were changing when she expressed the revolutionary view that the only hope of reforming dress was to start with children by educating them on the right lines from their early years. The Aesthetic Movement had a considerable part in shaping these new attitudes. 'If, at the end of the 'eighties, female dress reform had ceased to be a topical issue', says Stella Mary Newton in *Health, Art and Reason* (1974), her very full and perceptive study of nineteenth-century dress reform, 'comfortable, healthy, childlike dress for little boys and girls was widely approved, and this, too, was in tune with the spirit of the times.' The days of the worst child exploitation in industry were past, and the upbringing and education of the young were receiving increasing attention and thought. 'The "child of the period", a self-assured infant, began to appear in *Punch* and other journals with a sense of what was going on', comments Miss Newton.

There is, however, a perplexing contradiction in fashion trends for children in the 1880s and 1890s. Simultaneously 'aesthetic' dress was fostering loose, flowing, comfortable styles and was also giving a blessing and a stimulus to the fancy dress and uneasy 'period' costume which had been around for many years. What was the link between the two? Miss Newton suggests that it was the interest being taken by artists in children's dress. She instances an article, *Children's Dress in this Century*, written for *Women's World* in 1888 by Mrs Oscar Wilde, who said: 'It is probably owing to artists having turned their attention to matters of dress that we see so many picturesquely dressed children around us. Many of these dresses are historical, and the favourite dress for both boys and girls seems to be the Charles I dress. We have little Cavaliers in plush tunics and knickerbockers with coloured silk sashes and Vandyck collars.' But, she adds, 'plush is rather giving way to rough clothes for children's everyday dress . . . it seems scarcely suitable for the free physical

life that is so absolutely necessary for every healthy child.' Progress was being made. Nevertheless the two trends co-existed for many years.

Walter Crane (1845–1915), the famous illustrator of children's books, was, in addition to being a superb all-round decorative artist, also an educationalist, a Socialist and a dress reformer. He was the first president of the Art Workers' Guild, founded in 1884, was swept into the Socialist League by its founder and leading spirit William Morris, and in 1891 became Principal of the Royal College of Art.

He designed for young people the kind of clothes he thought combined utility, simplicity and picturesqueness, describing and drawing some of them in the journal *Aglaia* of the Healthy and Artistic Dress Union, which had a brief life in 1893–4. In it he shows a girl in a simple yoked dress with easy sleeves, loose neck and full skirt, plus a large, flat tam o'shanter cap. His boy alongside has loose knickerbockers, a loose belted jacket and a similar cap, while a small child who completes the group is similarly clad in easy, basic garments; all have short hair.

Lady Harberton disapproved of Kate Greenaway, the most famous of the artists who were influencing children's dress at this time. The Greenaway drawings were exact and meticulously produced versions of the dress of children at the turn of the century. Sometimes actual dresses were designed and made up by her, to be drawn on living models. They seemed to the

73 Children's clothes designed by Walter Crane and shown in *Aglaia*

74 Kate Greenaway's drawings
of children's clothes were
trendsetters

artist ideal. Not so to Lady Harberton, who declared that Miss Greenaway
'clothed the children of her fancy in "pretty" garments totally unsuited to
the practical needs and comforts of boys and girls.' She was all for plain
divided skirts for girls, and particularly disapproved of the ankle-length
Greenaway styles – with some reason. In spite of this the Greenaway cult
proved to be a long-lasting one, favoured by the artistic and helped by the
praise bestowed on the artist by John Ruskin for her 'minuteness and delicacy
of touch carried to the utmost limit.' Her influence in separating children's
fashions from adult styles and giving them simplicity of design and material
was substantial and lasting. Generations have loved her figures, but the
Greenaway styles were never generally adopted – though they have never
really disappeared. To this day they remain a favourite choice for the attire
of young bridesmaids and pages at smart weddings and little girls' party
dresses of the mid-1970s returned to the mode, even to the delicate sprigged
prints.

One of the most fervent of the Aesthetes was novelist and children's writer
E. Nesbit, Fabian, Bohemian, social worker, an 'advanced' woman and generally a bombshell. She was not only a lifelong wearer of aesthetic dress, often
made by herself, but she also put her daughters into it: 'I dress Iris in a kind
of loose gown now – it comes a little below her knees and she looks so aesthetic
and pretty in it. It is old gold colour. She has pinafores made after the same
pattern', she wrote in a letter in 1885, when the child was three or four. 'For
some years Aesthetic was to be one of her favourite adjectives of com-

mendation, and her little daughters, attired à la Kate Greenaway and Walter Crane, were to experience much embarrassment and discomfort among their school friends', comments her biographer, Doris Langley Moore. They had no say in what they wore and adult admiration did nothing to reconcile them to clothes they hated. 'Edith would go to sales', continues Mrs Langley Moore, 'and buy large quantities of fabrics which the children were compelled to wear out, and so uncommon . . . was their mother's taste, that they thought themselves very lucky if ever they were clad in ordinary garments.'

Liberty's also played a part in drawing children into the orbit of aesthetic dress reform in the 1880s and 1890s. Their lawns and other fine cottons, and their delicate designs were reminiscent of the 1800s. They issued two publications, both relevant to the development of children's dress at this time. *The Evolution of Costume*, which appeared in 1885, showed, for purposes of comparison, drawings of fashions of the 1800s and 1830s together with their modern adaptations. The more ambitious 1905 book had coloured fashion plates including a child's outfit inspired by Kate Greenaway.

Among the earliest and most devoted patrons of Arthur Lasenby Liberty, who opened his first shop, East India House, in Regent Street, in 1875, was Mary Eliza Haweis. She was a prolific and very gifted writer on fashion, a follower of the Aesthetic Movement and the pioneer of women interior decorators, whose efforts led to women taking a much wider part in the furnishing and décor of their homes. Inevitably her daughter, Hugolin, was dressed in the then fashionable aesthetic style, including the Kate Greenaway mode. But as usual the tastes of mother and daughter did not agree. Hugolin found the aesthetic clothes 'queer' and hated them, and when bright yellow stockings were added to her wardrobe 'their colour enraged her'. Her best moment came when 'much to her surprise, she had been given a nice plain holland smock to wear in the garden, and, when it blew, a red tam o'shanter. Her long, high-waisted Welbeck Street frock with its blue sash and hated bonnet which made people turn round and stare at her in the street, saying: "Quite a Kate Greenaway", had been put away till Christmas.'

This youthful disapproval must have been a sad blow for Hugolin's mother who in her book *The Art of Dress* (1879) had devoted a whole section to nursery hygiene and had urged that children should have distinctive clothes. 'She did not believe in copying adult fashions for them', says Bea Howe, her biographer. 'They should have special styles designed to meet their requirements.' As has been seen, Mrs Haweis's ideas of what these should be were very much of her time and place. Her son Lionel fared no better than her daughter so far as real reform was concerned. In 1878, when he was five or six, she wrote to her mother, saying that he 'has an early Charles II dress and an early English one. The first is made of crimson velvet slashed with white and trimmed with antique lace and sable, and the other is white blanketing trimmed with gold embroidery. He looks wonderful in both.' It is also recorded that 'Lionel . . . with his golden hair that stood out like a cloud from his head . . . had often been painted by his mother in his velvet suit with the lace collar.' What he thought of it all is not recorded!

Quite unchildlike colours continued to be worn by young children as the century drew towards its close. Compton Mackenzie, born in 1883 and

75 The revolution in girls' fashions was also fostered by Libertys in the 1890s. Here a style from their 1896 catalogue

76 Aesthetic frock for a four year old, 1890, with smocking and embroidery

a storehouse of remembered detail on what small boys wore in his time, recalls babyhood memories which extend remarkably far back to Glasgow, where 'I made my first appearance in a crimson pelisse and a ruby bonnet, a fore-runner of the LL.D's gown I should be given forty-seven years later.' He also recalls falling into a water butt at an early age, when his nanny 'took off my wet clothes and dressed me in my best frock of damson-coloured velvet with a lace collar.'

Moving on a few years to his first days at preparatory school at Colet Court, he recalls some clothes troubles. 'My next set-back was the discovery by an enemy that I was still wearing combinations when everybody else in the class wore pants and vest . . . Combinations carried with them the stigma of the nursery and even worse the stigma of femininity . . . There was another battle over a Norfolk suit. Other boys wore Norfolk suits of dark blue cloth. Why was I to be condemned to wear a conspicuous Norfolk suit of some Irish tweed my mother had brought home from Killarney, a suit so ridiculously conspicuous that Mr McDougall's favourites could always win a laugh by hailing me as "strawberry bags"?' His parents, professional actors, were no doubt influenced by the Aesthetic Movement. He also, however, wore sailor suits and had 'the white top of the ceremonial sailor-suit' for a prize-giving.

A flash-back to an earlier, more drab era is given in his description of a fellow-pupil. 'I can see Scott now. He wore a braided jacket and breeches of thick black rather shiny cloth. It must have been a suit his father had worn as a boy some thirty years before, which with Scottish thrift had been put away complete for possible wear in the future.' It was jeered at.

Interest in children's clothes was increasing towards the end of the century, but it was still being expressed in the form of much over-dressing of young people by proud mammas. 'Almost more interesting to a woman than her own clothes are those of her children', burbles Mrs Douglas, 'and perhaps nothing has more encouraged extravagance in this department than the recent furore for child-pictures, child-stories, child-heroes and child-actors. Some of our best *littérateurs* write fairy tales and collect poems for children, some of our best-known artists paint them, and the most serious minds are very solemnly concerning their wise nurture and education.' The 'furore' was to continue, and rightly so. The only surprising thing about it is her surprise, but the effects of it on clothes were to be quite different from her disapproving expectations.

Unexpectedly, signs of emancipation seem to have become evident in dresses for the very young while older boys were still uncomfortably clad. The *Queen* in 1890 wrote in the effusive style in which fashions were dealt with at the time: 'Nothing could be daintier for a damsel of one or two years old than a little smock of white washing silk . . . Another charming frock recalls the good little women and men in Hoppner's pictures, with its high-waisted slip of a bodice . . . Pretty blouse-waisted frocks for boys and girls are made either in pink, blue or white, smocked at the throat, and with the short skirt composed simply of a nine-inch flounce of embroidery.'

The mention of the colours perhaps gives a justifiable excuse for mentioning the tradition of 'blue for a boy, pink for a girl', which needs must puzzle any student of children's dress. It seems to have been widely observed during the last century, but how and when did it start? There is an isolated eighteenth-century reference in the Verney papers to a wedding for which 'pink coloured fringed gloves or white coloured lace gloves [are ordered] for a girl and sky coloured fringed gloves for a boy.' The choice of blue is believed to be associated with the old belief that evil spirits hovered over infants. Such spirits were thought to be allergic to certain colours, chief of them blue, because its association with the heavenly sky made evil spirits powerless before it. The wearing of blue by a young child was therefore a protection. As boys were much more important than girls, they needed special guarding, so blue was reserved for them. No such protection was thought necessary for girls, but later generations, unaware of the reason for the 'blue for a boy' but conscious of the omission of girls from any such distinction, thought up the idea of pink. Another European legendary tradition is quite different. It is that baby boys were found under cabbages, whose colour, in Europe, was mostly blue. Girls were born inside a pink rose.

77 No uniforms for the boys at the village school as shown in 1878 by C.O. Murray. Country smocks and a late version of the skeleton suit are included

9 School Uniforms

School uniforms have played a distinctive part in the evolution of children's dress, with affinities with both the fancy-dress trend and the Rational Dress Movement. Apart from the Tudor dress adopted in the sixteenth century for boys and girls, and in some cases retained to this day, such uniforms were late in developing. Records of them are also sparse and the study of the subject has only been broached surprisingly recently. It was in 1939 that the Rev. Wallace Clare in *The Historic Dress of the English Schoolboy* set out his aim as being 'to place on record for the first time annotated representations of a number of the many uniforms worn by English schoolboys since the sixteenth century.'

Rightly he singles out for detailed study the Eton suit, which is unique among school uniforms in combining a close identification with the school to which it belonged with a long and widespread general vogue among boys all over Britain and even in America. The Eton suit was, however, a fairly modern development. When the school was founded by Henry VI and got its charter in 1440, boys wore the long Tudor robes of the time, with a hood, supplied by the authorities as the school was originally a charitable foundation. These robes were worn for a long period, probably often over ordinary clothes of the current style. In 1478 Master Paston wrote home asking for 'a hose cloth, one for the holy days, of some colour, and another for the working days (how coarse soever it be maketh no matter), and a stomacher, and two shirts, and a pair of slippers.' In 1560 two sons·of Sir William Cavendish, aged ten and nine respectively, went to Eton and surviving bills show they wore gowns of black frieze and needed seven pairs of boots each in a year. Records relating to William Pitt, later Lord Chatham, at Eton in 1719, mention stockings, garters, mending thread, hatters, shoemakers' and tailors' bills but do not refer to uniform, according to H.C. Maxwell Lyte, who in 1875 wrote the first comprehensive book on the history of the college.

The Rev. Wallace Clare ascribes the origin of the Eton suit to the late eighteenth century. He identifies the jacket with the short style, without lapels, worn by small boys at that time and the trousers with those also first introduced as part of the skeleton suit. He says that a portrait of a boy wearing such a suit was painted in 1798 and that originally the trousers buttoned on to the shirt, as in the skeleton suit. There was, however, no uniformity at this time. Oppidans were wearing trousers by 1814 but Collegers continued to wear breeches for some years after this. An autograph manuscript *Etonian*, treasured in the Eton College library and written by Edward Coleridge, a first cousin of the poet, who went to Eton in May 1813, tells that 'at the time the boys generally dressed in blue cloth coats and trousers and pale yellow waistcoats . . . Any boy appearing in black was known to be in mourning.'

78 The Eton suit took priority in an advertisement in *Punch* of 'child styles' of 1892

"ETON."   "EDINBORO'."   "NORFOLK."   "JACK TAR."   "CHESTERFIELD."   "PRINCE."

This refutes the oft-repeated assertion that the black Eton jacket was adopted in place of blue and red ones in 1818 on the death of George III, who took a great interest in the college. This claim is also denied by today's college authorities and by J.D.R. McConnell who, in *Eton and How it Works* (1967), states: 'It is a fallacy that the costume of the present day Etonian represents mourning for George III. The uniform came into being in the nineteenth century when it was felt that some curb must be placed on the individual eccentricities of boys' dress. The clothing adopted for all was a sort of lowest common denominator of a gentleman's dress in the London of the period. Of course it looks odd' – because it is now a bygone fashion.

The persistence of variations in dress at Eton is also recorded in *Seven Years at Eton, 1857–1864*, which says that 'The new boy would come with a coloured cravat tied in a bow, a stick-up collar, or a brown jacket with gold buttons. . . . Boys often came strangely attired, because their fathers who had been to Eton retained vague recollections of the latitude that existed about Costume in the days of Montem, when the scarlet tail coats worn by the Fifth form boys, and the blue jackets with white ducks donned by the Lower ones, were sported afterwards through the summer-half till used up. Even now odd mistakes are made about Eton attire. I lately saw in *Punch* some drawings in which Eton fellows were introduced wearing jackets with neckties *in a bow*. What was F.C. Burnand about when he forgot that the black cravat of the boy in jackets had to be tied in a sailor's knot, while the white one of a boy in coats or tails was equally bound to take the shape of a bow?' Uniform had taken over with a vengeance.

The ancient Montem procession seems to have given a lead to the introduction of uniforms at Eton, and its special costume is recorded fully in the picture gallery at the college, and also by actual examples of these uniforms, worn by boys in 1793 and 1844 – almost identical red tail coats, white breeches and frilled shirts. The last Montem was in 1846, and from that time the boys' clothing made steady progress towards a uniformity similar to that of today. The Eton picture gallery is rich in pictures showing boys of last century in variations of this attire. Top hats are seen in 1838, and on the river in 1852. Cricketers of the latter year wear top hats, short jackets and trousers of grey, fawn or white, in accordance with the contemporary fashions for men. A number of water-colour scenes by William Evans (1798–1877), a drawing master at the College for many years, show a wide variety of clothing worn by boys taking part in various games.

For the great 4 June boats event fancy dress was worn to start with, but by about 1814, H.C. Maxwell Lyte says, this was abandoned and a regular uniform was adopted, similar to that still worn in 1875: 'It consisted of a dark blue cloth jacket, a striped or checked shirt of some distinctive pattern, a straw hat bearing the name of the Boat, and trousers of dark blue cloth for the boys in the Upper Boats, and of white jean for those in the Lower Boats. The Steerers continued to wear fancy dress of their own choosing until 1828, when they too adopted a regular uniform, viz: that of officers in the Royal Navy, Lieutenants, Captains and Admirals, according to the precedence to which their respective boats were entitled.'

The Eton suit for small boys was well established by 1860, according to numerous records. 'Tradition, old prints and the memory of men still alive make it clear that long before 1860 all boys wore clothes which did not differ fundamentally from those in use at the present day', say L.R.S. Byrne and E.L. Churchill in *Changing Eton* (1937). Photographs, they add, 'show that the dark coat and waistcoat with either a turn-down or stick-up collar, or the Eton jacket and Eton collar were as much *de rigeuer* then as now.' The Eton collar was derived from the broad turn-down cambric collar still worn by boys in the first half of the nineteenth century. The tall hat, a feature of several public schools, was first introduced to Eton in 1820, replacing the mortar-board previously worn.

The main point about the Eton suit was that while fashions in jackets changed and a loose, rounded style became popular for boys during the 1860s and later, Eton boys retained the style they were to make famous. It was, in fact, a prime example of a uniform being a fossilized fashion, as often happens in that area of dress. It was also something more, being the only example which exists of a specific school uniform becoming a general youthful fashion. The Eton suit was copied everywhere. The proudest achievement of

79 Eton collars worn by all the boys at Stratford Board School in 1899, with Norfolk jackets, below the knee 'shorts' and clumsy boots

mothers in all walks of life was to dress their sons, once out of the Fauntleroy stage, in Eton suits for Sunday best and for parties. Advertisements in magazines and newspapers of the latter part of last century feature the Eton suit as a general fashion and America was as avid for it as was Britain. A personal record of one small girl's admiration for the suit comes from Eleanor Sillar who, writing of Edinburgh in the early 1880s, recalls her hero worship of the boys of the nearby Cargilfield school: 'I stand and gaze, adoring them in their Eton suits and little top-hats, each with a huge unrolled umbrella as tall as himself.' In more detail she continues: 'The legs were clothed in grey trousers and the Eton jackets were very short.' At church all that she could see was 'rows upon rows of curly heads and Eton collars', but better was to come. Her 'proudest moment was eventually knowing a boy in an Eton suit.' It seems very remote now, but in fact the vogue for the Eton suit lasted until the present century and the Eton collar achieved a prestige of its own, being worn with other types of suits by young boys of all classes. The Eton collar features regularly in Army and Navy store catalogues of the 1890s. Young choristers at some of our cathedrals still wear Eton suits.

Perhaps the oddest thing about the Eton suit was that the word was also used to describe women's suits. There is a description in 1894 of a lady riding 'in an Eton suit and blue sailor hat' and in *Sylvia Scarlett* (1918) Compton Mackenzie writes: 'Sylvia was wearing Etons at Monkley's suggestion.' Oddest of all, perhaps, was the female Eton crop, that short hair-cut of the emancipated woman of the 1920s. Edgar Wallace in *The Square Emerald* in 1926 describes a woman character: 'The masculinity of the powerful face was emphasized by the grey hair, cut close in an Eton crop', which was then a new fashion. *Punch* mentions the same style in 1930 and in 1958 Beverley Nichols in his nostalgic *Sweet and Twenties* describes a woman of the 1920s: 'She is an Eton-cropped . . . mannish young woman'. The Oxford Dictionary includes the style in its 1933 supplement as 'a fashion of cutting women's hair close to the head all over'. Why Eton should be associated with this is not clear; the fact that by its charter of 1440 the college forbade boys to wear long hair seems to be going too far back for credibility.

Prestige and comfort tend to lie at opposite extremes in costume, as in other things, and it could scarcely be claimed that the prestigious Eton suit was designed for ease. With its accompanying top hat and stiffly starched collar it is extremely inhibiting by today's standards, but other developments in school uniforms were moving in a freer direction. This was mainly due to the fact that most of them for both boys and girls originated as sports clothes. The rise of organized games was part of the development of public and then of other schools. Team games called for team clothes, as was detailed at the end of *Tom Brown's Schooldays*, when Tom achieved the captaincy of the cricket team and saw uniformity of dress attained. On his last day at school, aged 19, he was resplendent 'in white flannel shirt and trousers, straw hat, the Captain's belt, and the untanned yellow cricket shoes which all the eleven wear.' Arthur, at his feet, is 'similarly dressed'. School caps copied cricket caps, and the flannels worn by generations of schoolboys derived from cricket flannels and were worn with blazers which also had a sporting origin.

The team sprit became highly important in later nineteenth-century school life, and the moral and psychological effect of uniforms was strongly stressed. The process by which this happened is described effectively by Arthur Ponsonby in *The Decline of the Aristocracy*, published in 1912, but curiously prophetic of today's reaction from the regimented sport which was so popular at that time. 'Compare a photograph of a group of schoolboys of today with one of only 40 to 50 years ago. The comparison is instructive. In the latter boys will be seen lounging about in different attitudes with a curious variety of costumes. If it is a football eleven they will be in varied and strange garments, with their trousers tucked into their socks, some bareheaded, some with ill-fitting caps and old shrunken shirts, others perhaps neater, but each one individual and distinct. The group today consists of two or three rows of boys beautifully turned out with immaculate, perfectly fitting clothing. In the football eleven each will wear a cap, shirt, shoes, stockings of precisely the same pattern. They stand and sit so that the line of the peaks of their caps, of their folded arms, of their bare knees is mathematically level. And even their faces! You can hardly tell one from another . . . Now no one will say that this can be accounted for by the improvement in the tailor's art and an artistic desire for regularity in the photographer. It is . . . an outward and visible sign . . . of the stereotyping and conventionalizing effect of our modern educational system. This stereotyping . . . constitutes perhaps the strongest indictment that has yet to be brought against our Public Schools.' Bold words for the time.

Other writers note the same uniformity in clothes as 'a significant change which, to judge by the actual photographs of teams and masters, began to take place in the 1860s in many schools . . . but it was another 20 years or more before it was firmly and generally established.' Up to 1875, Byrne and Churchill point out, 'football was still played in any old trousers, and boys went to games in tails or Eton jackets. In the next decade trousers were cut down to knickerbockers, with straps and buckles below the knees. Between 1880 and 1890 shorts superseded knickerbockers, being optional at first and later the privilege of those representing their House for football. Since 1932 shorts have been worn by all.'

It is curious that this uniformity among schoolboys, stemming from sport, coincides in time with the adoption of something like 'uniforms' among men – dark suits, first with frock or morning coats, then culminating in the almost universal lounge suit of the business man and the disappearance for nearly a century of colour and variety from the once peacock-proud male wardrobe. But contrariwise the adoption of school uniforms by girls round about the same time led to no such corresponding change in women's clothes, but merely to a growing divergence between the attire of girls and women for more than a generation.

A surprisingly early description of schoolgirl games uniform occurs in the novel of the 1860s, *Comin' Through the Rye*, already referred to. The narrator, sent to boarding school for disciplinary reasons, is getting ready for her first game of cricket, which 'had flourished for many years' at the school. 'In 30 seconds the room is cleared, and we are all upstairs . . . and putting on knickerbockers and blouses! *Yes, knickerbockers!* Let no one blush or look shocked, for they are long and ample, and tied modestly in at the ankle; and as to the blouse, which descends below the knee, and is trimly belted in at the waist . . . our costume being, in short, nothing more or less than that which is designated by the somewhat opprobrious title of "Bloomer". The knicker-bockers bring comfort, the tunic confers respectability.' Girls are all 'shrunken insignificant creatures, measured by the standard of half an hour ago, when they boasted a circumference of from four to five yards of petticoat.'

The bicycle enjoys chief credit for bringing the idea of freedom and comfort into women's fashions for the first time when it swept into popularity in the 1890s, but schoolgirls' clothes anticipated the machine. The reformers, as a century before, were educationalists and they came mainly from the band of pioneer headmistresses who, in the second half of the nineteenth century, revolutionized girls' education. They not only set up schools from which pupils could proceed to the slowly opening doors of the universities and the

80　Four sisters of 1890 dressed in the fashion of the time: surprisingly, no gloves

81 No uniforms for these
school girls at Wolvey in 1896

professions but they also established games and gymnastics as part of a guiding principle of '*mens sana in corpore sano*'. For such activities the female clothes of the time were quite unsuitable.

Frances Mary Buss (1827–94), first of the new-style headmistresses, was also the first to introduce a system of gymnastics for all and to make a move towards suitable dress for this activity. The North London Collegiate School for Ladies, as it was first called when she founded it in 1850 on the basis of an earlier school started with her mother in 1845 when she was 18, was always forward-looking. In 1868 she wrote in a letter to a lady in Otago, which was published in a colonial newspaper: 'No school ought to omit *physical training* – that is Callisthenics – or some equivalent. Our system, an American idea, called Musical Gymnastics, is excellent. Easy, graceful and not too fatiguing, gently calling every part of the body into play . . . it has become popular, and has wonderfully improved the figure and carriage of the girls.' When the school, now for 'Girls', was rebuilt and opened by the Prince of Wales in 1873, it included a gymnasium, 'a splendid room a hundred feet long, and about forty feet high', where there were regular daily classes and longer periods twice a week for all.

For these activities the restricting, heavily corseted girls' dress of the time was obviously unsuitable, and dress reform found a strong advocate in Miss Buss. Her friend and biographer, Annie E. Ridley, recorded that 'suitable clothing was also a matter of careful consideration. Miss Buss would have liked a school uniform which she would have made graceful as well as rational,

82   The need for reform in
children's clothes for active life
is underlined by this fashion
plate of a seaside scene of 1886
from *Le Journal des Enfants*

but except in the gymnasium, she never attained this desire, and had to content herself advising . . . She waged war against unsuitable ornamentation, lace and jewellery in the morning being always attacked.' A pupil of the 1880s recalled in a centenary tribute to Miss Buss the regular compulsory classes in the gymnasium, a demonstration given before Queen Victoria at the 1884 Health Exhibition and how she was 'very proud of my blue jersey and skirt and wide red sash round my middle.' Other recollections were that 'we were not allowed to wear dresses below the ankle', that tight clothing was disapproved of, corsets condemned and clothes hanging from the shoulders strongly advocated.

There was a famous day in 1890 when the games captain, Ethelda Budgett-Meakin, persuaded Miss Buss to introduce Olympic games and competitions in a field at Epping hired for the occasion. This was unheard-of for girls at the time. Unfortunately it rained, so the sports had to be held in the Town Hall, but according to the School Magazine 'each girl wore a light coloured skirt reaching only to her knees, a white blouse loosely belted at the waist, a cap either blue striped (arts) or red striped (science).' This was startling for the time. Subsequently Sports became an annual event, but were held in the school gymnasium. There still exist copies of the school magazine for 1891 and 1892 recording how the girls appeared 'some in full gymnasium costume, others in short, bright-coloured skirts and white blouses' in 1891. In 1892 'there were several new features. First as to costume – everyone wore short skirts and white blouses, with yellow or blue sashes, according as they were partisans of the old or new Universities.'

Dorothea Beale (1831–1906), indissolubly linked with Miss Buss in the cause of girls' education, taught for a year at Casterton, the original of Lowood in *Jane Eyre*, where even in her time 'the pupils wore a hideous uniform which seemed to her to emphasize the petty restrictions which encompassed them and which gave her a permanent horror of regimentation and a dislike of school uniforms.' It did not, however, stop her from advocating dress reform when she became the first headmistress of Cheltenham Ladies College in 1858. She offered to show parents 'various harmless substitutes for stays' and also for boots and shoes with pointed toes and high heels. She put a ban on any stays that could easily be tightened and advocated wool next to the skin both in summer and winter. She established the biggest and best playing fields in existence for girls, even though, watching her girls battling for the ball at hockey, she issued the command: 'Get them some more balls at once.' She was also one of the first to introduce the straw boater as a school fashion, giving a countrywide lead in this respect.

Dame Louisa Lumsden, the most dynamic of the five pioneer students who blazed the trail to Girton by forming the nucleus of an unofficial college at Hitchen and from there passing the Cambridge degree examinations, was the first headmistress of St Leonards, the first girls' school to be set up on the lines of a boys' public school. There she was an early advocate of dress reform during her five years' reign from 1877 to 1882. 'Dress', she said long afterwards in her memoirs *Yellow Leaves*, 'may seem a trifling thing, but even from childish days it had worried me. I wanted to be free to run, jump and climb trees.' When the opportunity came to liberate a younger generation

83 Sailor blouses and boys' caps for the cricket team at Roedean in 1902

she did so by introducing a games uniform of which the main features were a blue knee-length tunic worn over knickerbockers or trousers. At first these could be of any length, but they were soon standardized just below the knee and a dark blue serge tunic, with a leather or webbing belt, and knickerbockers to match, were worn for many years. Tam o'shanters were also worn, and the straw sailor hat of generations of schoolgirls had an early reign here (though probably originating at Cheltenham Ladies' College). It was first worn at St Leonards in 1887, under Dame Louise Lumsden's successor, Miss, later Dame, Frances Dove who, at a picnic at Rumbling Bridge, noted the variegated attire of her girls and decided that headgear at least could be uniform even away from the games fields. A cloak worn out of doors was adapted, according to Miss Dove, who introduced it, from a style worn by peasants of the Pas de Calais area.

Of this early uniform of St Leonards one wearer wrote much later that 'in 1877 the girls in this school actually wore, in their own grounds a dress assimilating in essentials to the ordinary dress of the girls and women of today.' The fact that the first school uniforms were ahead of contemporary fashions was probably one reason why they were somewhat slowly adopted for general school wear, being confined to the gymnasium at many schools until the start of the present century.

Some early sports outfits for schoolgirls took their inspiration from those of boys. Thus shirt blouses with stiff collars, worn with serge skirts were worn by early hockey and cricket teams and were at times completed by boys' caps. In adopting skirts and blouses girls gave the lead to women, who did not take to this fashion until the end of the century, when the tailor-made suit and a shirt with stiff collar (the least comfortable item of the male wardrobe) were worn by the New Woman in her emancipated mood. Roedean girls wore another boy-inspired sports outfit in the shape of a sailor suit, or rather a sailor blouse, complete with striped dickey, and a skirt.

The gym tunic, by far the most famous of all items of girls' school uniform for more than half a century, is somewhat difficult to trace back to its beginnings, in this country at least. Its originator is stated by Phillis Cunnington and Alan Mansfield in their *English Costume for Sport and Outdoor Recreation* to have been Madame Bergman Osterberg, a Swedish teacher. As head of the Dartford College for Physical Training, she introduced it in 1885 for gymnastics. After that time it seems to have been worn extensively, and a photograph of a Scottish schoolgirl of about 1890 shows the style worn with a leg-of-mutton sleeved blouse of the day.

There are many references at this time to the wearing of the djibbah for gymnastics. It is recorded as being worn at Roedean at the end of last century and as having been designed for that school by a professional dress designer, who based it on the dress of North African tribesmen, as she told Miss Millicent Lawrence, one of the pioneer sisters who started the famous school. There is also a description of a 1904 St Paul's schoolgirl, 'Pauline Hockney, clad in the blue djibbah of her time, with white blouse made by herself in School.' St Paul's dropped the djibbah in 1906, taking to skirts and blouses for games until 1915, when gym tunics were adopted.

What was the djibbah like? Phillis Cunnington and Anne Buck say that the Roedean djibbah, 'a knee-length dress with a round neck and short sleeves,

84   The schoolgirl 'boater' made an early appearance at St Leonards where it is worn by a sketching party in 1899, and also by the teacher

fitted the figure fairly closely and flared out from the hips without pleats.' The djibbah, they continue, 'had no general popularity; indeed the typical gym tunic had no serious rival for hockey players until it was ousted at last by shorts.' The Costume Museum at Bath has a djibbah corresponding to this description to some degree, but it is waistless. Another, with a waist and flaring skirt, has tight sleeves and is ankle-length and near-adult-size.

There is an odd reference to the djibbah in a passage in Enid Bagnold's autobiography, published in 1969, in which she recalls her schooldays at Prior's Field, the school for girls run by Mrs Leonard Huxley: 'We wore games "djibbahs", with scarlet sashes. The large box pleats, which should have hung straight from the yoke, were pulled apart from my breasts. I looked like the top drawer of a chest of drawers pulled out.' Box pleats are hard to reconcile with the dress of African tribesmen!

The gym tunic, usually of navy-blue serge, was in truth not flattering to the adolescent girl who ran to puppy fat or whose figure was developing curves. Nevertheless, it remained in favour and became a general school uniform for many years. In design its significance was that it was the first time for centuries that the full weight of feminine costume had hung from the shoulders, leaving the waist completely free. Its advocates also banned corsets, and nothing more than a straight, unconstricting bodice was worn under it. At first baggy bloomers were its accompaniment, but by the second decade of this century these were superseded by 'gym tights' – closely fitting navy-blue wool knickers, usually in a ribbed weave. Stockings were still usually kept up by garters, though sometimes under-bodices had suspenders attached to them. But some enterprising schoolgirls of the 1920s gave a fashion lead to the 1960s when, 'for special occasions', according to one report, 'long black stockings were sewn to knitted tights to avoid a gap known as a "smile".' It was the birth of today's stocking tights.

Sara Burstall, another of the headmistresses who left their mark on their pupils' clothing as well as on their education, presided over Manchester High School for Girls for many years. She recalled in her memoirs *Retrospect and Prospect* in 1937 how difficult it had been to introduce uniforms at the start of the century. Even hat-bands offended parents; 'In 1902, however, we made an attempt to introduce the minimum of school uniform, and were met at once by a host of difficulties. Some mothers said that the school colour did not suit the girls' complexions, and others objected as they thought the uniform hat the badge of a charity school, and a social degradation. It was impossible to find any shape of hat which would suit everyone, and every style was open to objections. We had to go very slowly at first and it was a very long time before the uniform gymnastic tunic, so popular today, became possible with us.' But, she continues, 'the wearing of a suitable school dress was made very much easier through the influence of a new system of gymnastics, which came to us in 1900. This was the eclectic one in use in the Frances Mary Buss schools, a combination of German and Swedish methods, but with music.'

To the girls uniforms were not always unwelcome, whatever parents might think. Winifred Peck in *A Little Learning* looked back on early days at Wycombe Abbey, modelled on St Leonards and staffed by many teachers from that school. The headmistress Miss Frances Dove, also late of St Leonards,

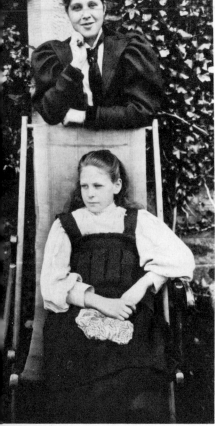

85   Gym tunic of the 1890s

had grown up in the Buss–Beale tradition, but felt that they devoted too much time and attention to brain-work and not enough to wider interests. To redress this, she gave more attention to games and, says Winifred Peck, 'part of the fun came from the games dress – short tunics and baggy bloomers, with tam o'shanters which always fell off.' Miss Dove would have liked to abolish corsets, but mothers would have made an outcry, so 'of stiff buckram and heavy boned they constricted our plump frames, except at games, and added to our sartorial tortures when bones broke and plunged into our sides.'

Although uniforms were still at a tentative stage at the end of last century, they represented a considerable degree of emancipation for the time. An 1892 schoolgirl recalled: 'Our long black stockings, hitched up like tights, very short pleated blue serge skirts, a long woven jersey, was the only uniform the school indulged in' – but that was far from current adult fashions with their rigid upholstered lines.

10 A Slow Start for the 'Century of the Child'

That the 'century of the child' should have begun punctually in 1900 would be beyond all logic, both as regards the clothes which were to symbolize it and the new attitudes which were to be one of the main factors influencing what children wore. For infants above all the approach of the turn of the century produced no signs of liberation and the long, cumbersome, many-layered clothes of their first months continued in the Victorian tradition. Binders, shawls, pelisses, bonnets, veils, long robes and long flannels and even stiffened and quilted staybands all pressed upon the babe almost from birth.

An 1888 layette, described in J.E. Panton's *From Kitchen to Garret: Hints for Young Householders*, includes '12 very fine lawn shirts, 10 long flannels . . . 6 fine long cloth petticoats, 8 monthly gowns . . . 8 nightgowns, 4 head flannels, a large flannel shawl, 6 dozen large Russian diapers, 6 good flannel pilches, 3 or 4 pairs tiny woollen shoes.' A formidable list, surely planned for more than the first few weeks of the infant's life. A Dickins and Jones catalogue of 1895 includes in a layette both flannel and cotton swathes and a diversity of elaborately trimmed garments. Flannel bands and cotton and webbing swathes are featured in another catalogue of the 1890s of a leading Piccadilly shop, C & A Quitman.

In real life Prof. J.B.S. Haldane, born in 1890, is recorded by his mother as having, as a small boy, protested to nursemaids he met in the road about their babies being so wrapped up and having their faces veiled. She does not say whether he protested when 'I kept his lint-white locks until he went to school', as was also usual at the time. The bright hair and curls of the small boy seem to have roused much more rapture among mothers than the presumably equally usual ones of girls. In real life, again, in the annual medical report of the Uxbridge Urban District Council of 1906, the Medical Officer of Health, Dr D.L. Lock put forward various recommendations regarding the care of infants and young children, because the infant death rate had been very high there at the beginning of the twentieth century. These included: 'A flannel binder should be worn round the stomach and abdomen next to the skin; it should be sufficiently wide to cover the whole belly from hips to chest, and long enough to go twice round the body.' It remained in use until at least the 1920s, despite the reformers.

It was also still customary about this time for boys to wear dresses until they were four or more years old. A photograph of the late King George VI

86 Little liberation for the small boy of 1900, still encumbered by dresses abounding in frills and flounces, lace and embroidery

87   King George VI in a sailor
dress, right, with the Duke of
Windsor, sailor-suited, the
Princess Royal, and their
Mother, Queen Mary

as a small boy shows him in a sailor dress with a pleated skirt. Osbert Sitwell, born in 1892, recalls in *Left Hand Right Hand* a childhood dominated by the sailor suit from early years, with photographs of himself thus attired at the ages of three, four and six. Before that it was dresses for boys. For a Sargent family portrait painted when he was seven his father chose the clothes for all, with 'myself in a sailor suit, with white duck trousers, while Sacheverell wore a silk dress suitable for his age', which was then more than three years. The custom died hard. Lord Clark the art historian, born in 1903, is pictured in his autobiography as a small boy in a dress, long black stockings and a big tam o'shanter. His family moved in fashionable circles. Graham Greene, born in 1904, recalls in his autobiography *A Sort of Life* an early episode: 'My age was then about four, and I wore a pinafore, and had fair curls falling around the neck. My elder brother with a proper masculine haircut, an adult of seven, stares fearlessly towards the box-camera . . . while I still have the ambiguity of undetermined sex.'

In 1907 the curator of Eton College is on record as declaring: 'Petticoats for small boys are to be recommended in every way. The putting of infants at an early age into woollen knickerbocker suits cannot but be bad for them physically.' A real-life confirmation of this mode of dress comes in *The Oppidan*, Shane Leslie's 'Eton novel based on memories of boys and masters of the turn of the century.' It records a recollection of Miss Evans, a famous Eton dame, about a boy who, in her early days, 'came to Eton very young, because his parents went to India. . . . I remember him standing in petticoats at the bottom of the stairs. I was a strong young girl, and I carried him up under my arm.' That must have been last century, but it still is none the less startling in an Eton context.

Compton Mackenzie, still chronicling what he wore as he grew out of early childhood, tells that, moving up to St Paul's in 1894, when he was eleven, he went to Barker's 'for my first Eton jacket, Sunday top hat, and various other articles of clothing.' Then 'in one's seventeenth year . . . one was privileged to give up wearing the school cap, don a bowler, and carry one's books under the arm instead of in a bag.' He recalls Cecil Chesterton at fifteen 'still wearing an Eton jacket which he was much too bulky to become', and Leonard Woolf, in another recollection, 'must by now have been fully sixteen, yet he was still in an Eton jacket and looked not a day more than fourteen.' The appointed dress was not always acceptable to the less privileged: 'One's Sunday top-hat was a continuous object of derision, and even the straw-hats we wore in summer with our Eton jackets drew shouts behind us of "straw-yard straw-yard". The word "boater" was never used . . . "boater" was intended to suggest to maid-servants that they were as familiar with Maidenhead as Gaiety Girls.' A photograph of the author aged fourteen shows him in straw hat, Eton collar, wide knotted tie, but jacket and waistcoat of tweed, not the Eton jacket. At 16 he has a high, stiff double collar, patterned tie and lounge suit.

Of freedom to come the only real evidence in the attire of the boy of about 1900 was that about this time shorts began to be worn by older boys – the very young wore them in the latter part of the nineteenth century. Now shorts were gradually adopted – and shorts that revealed bare knees, not the previous chopped-off trousers worn with long stockings. Shorts seem to have started, like most of the liberating clothes of children, on the playing fields. At Eton, about the turn of the present century, only those who played football for their House were allowed to be bare-kneed, the others still wearing knickerbockers, but this privilege was extended soon afterwards and shorts became general. The further development of shorts is, however, a later story.

Girls' clothes, which had followed the extravagances of those of women's fashions very closely from about the 1830s, had broken away from this tend towards the end of the nineteenth century, spurred on, as has been explained, by two new elements – the Aesthetic Movement and the development of education on lines which called for dress suitable for the newly introduced

88   In spite of liberating
influences, the fashionable
Edwardian small girl still
suffered from some of the
extravagancies of her mother's
modes, as seen in this fashion
plate from *The Queen* in 1900

gymnastics and organized outdoor games. Though there was a certain link between the two influences, not only in the people who advocated them but also in the injection into dress of ideas of health and comfort, for some time this did not influence fashion. It took the form of a growing difference between clothes of schoolgirls and of women, especially fashionable women. The Edwardian lady, with her exaggerated bust, flowing hips, tightly constricted waistline aided by her S-shaped corset, and her frou-frou of elaborate petticoats round her feet, bore little resemblance to the contemporary girl in gym dress or sports skirt and shirt blouse, or in her loose, simple dresses hanging from the shoulders and often smocked peasant-style. Magazines of the time, increasingly aimed at the women's market, show girls in easy, unrestricting dress in illustrations. *Woman at Home*, edited by best-selling novelist Annie S. Swan, is typical. The children in E. Nesbit's books, in the original illustrations by H.R. Miller at the start of the century, also wear easy clothes, including sailor suits ana dresses, loose frocks, pinafores and casual tam o'shanters, with no aping of their mothers' modes. Though the New Woman was being talked about, her clothes remained restricting and unnatural in shape. It was young girls who led the way to the freedom to come – and mainly middle-class girls going to their day schools and leading the way to future middle-class fashion domination.

That freedom applied to girls' everyday clothes, but there was also in the early twentieth century a great vogue for elaborate, heavily starched white muslin, lawn, piqué and other kinds of cotton dresses, often embroidered and lace-trimmed, for party, best and Sunday wear. With such dresses inevitably went white petticoats and knickers, also much trimmed. There were also coats of white piqué and elaborate bonnets and hats, likewise of cotton with lace or embroidery to bedeck them, and all of them much starched. These were mainly confined to smaller girls, but they were by no means limited to the rich. Despite their upkeep in terms of washing and ironing, they were worn by children of all but the poorest classes, including many whose mothers must have had to toil over the wash-tub and ironing board to produce this symbol of their self-respect, their pride in their family and their social aspirations. Keeping clean must have been at times a sore trial to the wearers, but many little girls revel in finery and emulation in dress is a human trait from which they are not immune. The idea that they should set their own fashions had not yet been born.

89 The ordinary small girl was dressed in starched white from top to toe in 1909, but evidently did not approve of her frilly bonnet – or gloves

Innovations did begin to come into children's dress from the early twentieth century. A notable one, both in itself and as the harbinger of trends to come, was the America-inspired Buster Brown suit for small boys, which first became popular about 1908. It was based on the attire of a character in a comic strip drawn by an American artist, Richard Foutcault, for a Sunday newspaper, which had a wide following among American children. Such strips, part of the growing attention being given to children, had originated about the end of the previous century, with Britain's *Chips* and *Comic Cuts* both starting in 1890, and Weary Willie and Tired Tim, created by artist Tom Browne, becoming favourite characters with generations of boys.

Buster Brown was, however, the first imaginary character to influence boys'

dress substantially since little Lord Fauntleroy. The outfit that bore his name
consisted of a suit with bloomer-style, wide, knee-length pants, a double-
breasted hip-length belted jacket with a round neck, worn with a wide,
starched collar and a black floppy bow and completed by a round straw hat.
There was even a Buster Brown shoe, a new style which 'correctly shaped the
growing foot while giving style to the shoe', according to Madge Garland in
The Changing Face of Childhood. With it also went short hair, with a fringe.
The whole ensemble became highly popular in Britain as well as in its native
America – the first of a rising tide of American fashions to come.

When, in 1908, Paul Poiret introduced into Paris fashion a straight up-
and-down line that followed the natural female figure and put an end for
ever to the artificial shaping which had prevailed throughout fashion for
centuries, with the brief exception of the child-inspired simplicity of the late
1700s and early 1800s, he was not thinking of the young. But he brought
adult women's fashions nearer to those of contemporary children in that he
aimed at freedom in most respects – even though his 'hobble' skirt brought a
new restriction, a final gesture of snobbery, since only the leisured and rich
could wear it in its undiluted form. It had, however, only a brief vogue for
a few pre-war years and even then often had a slit or pleats to make it wearable
by the active woman.

He claimed to have banished the corset, as dress reformers and school-
mistresses had been trying to do for more than a generation. He did not
literally succeed, but he did rid the fashion world of the heavily boned, waist-
constricting corsets which had been the foundations of fashion for centuries,
afflicting young girls and even boys as well as adults with the evils of tight-
lacing. Above all, he inaugurated a new way of thinking about fashion in
terms of the natural figure, of the young and the active. Fashion plates of the
years before World War I played its part in this process show small girls
wearing clothes that follow the new lines. It is also notable that children's
clothes of the time featured the hip-line 'waist' that was to dominate women's
fashions of the 1920s. Little girls also had, about 1913, skirts that were almost
hip-high, years before women shortened their dresses. It was the first move of
fashion towards the young, instead of being directed at the mature woman
whose opulent curves had been the Edwardian ideal but which were never
again to come into favour.

It is probably a coincidence, but none the less a significant fact, that the year
1908 also saw the introduction of one of the greatest innovations in girls'
underwear – the Liberty bodice, rightly so described and universally acclaimed
for more than a generation. It was created by the famous, old-established and
still flourishing corset firm, Symingtons of Market Harborough. It was a
soft front-buttoning bodice made of finely knitted cotton stockinette in the
then usual 'natural' colour, kept in shape not by the usual bones or stiffening
but by bands of tape. In a few years it became world-famous, ousting the
previous styles of stay-bands and bodices. Output soared and reached a total
of 3,500,000 a year. In 1925 a light version, the 'Peter Pan' fleecy bodice, was
introduced and was also very successful. The Liberty bodice ruled the schoolgirl's foundation wear until the 1950s, when the 'youth revolution' and the
great new developments in fabrics and designs in this area brought in new

90 Freedom comes into girls' wear, as shown by this Jaeger advertisement for November 1909

91 A new era in children's underwear was symbolized by Chilprufe. The trade mark was registered about 1911, with this cheerful figure used on advertisements for many years

concepts. But versions of it still exist.

World War I put vast numbers of women into uniforms as they took over men's jobs for the first time in history and in 1916–17, also for the first time, they were enrolled in their own newly created uniformed sections of the army, navy and air force. The innovation in dress was for many of them not so revolutionary as it might have been, because most of these young women had been accustomed to school uniforms and to school disciplines at work and at games. For those still children during the war there were also many changes. It was, in the main, the end of the long era of frilly knickers and starched, flounced petticoats, of fancy white party dresses with sashes. Girls now wore bloomers to match their dresses, usually sensibly coloured, gave up petticoats for the most part, and wore plainer clothes. The gym tunic became general school uniform in many cases, and in others the most usual everyday wear was navy blue serge pleated skirts, buttoned on to cotton bodices and worn with woollen jerseys or plain cotton or Viyella blouses, gathered into elastic at the waist and completed by school ties. Navy blue reefer jackets were worn with this outfit.

New at this time and easily distinguished by her appearance was the flapper, who anticipated the much-talked of Teenage era or Youth Revolution by about 40 years and was the first harbinger of things to come. She reached the limelight during and after World War I, but was born before 1914. In the autumn of 1975 a considerable and entertaining correspondence in the *Daily Telegraph* brought her out of near-oblivion, at the instigation of Miss H.M. Drennan, who set out to correct the idea that the 1920s were the decade of the flapper. As one of the original group now 'over or pushing eighty', she refuted this by the firm statement that 'I, as an ex-flapper, should know' that the years of the flapper were 'before and a little after 1914.'

The flapper was aged from about 15 to 18. She wore her skirts enticingly shorter than adults of the time; had as her hall-mark the large upstanding taffeta ribbon bows she wore on her long, tied-back hair or long plaits. This was an extreme version of a contemporary schoolgirl fashion which belonged to the days of pig-tails and other long-hair styles. Every self-respecting girl took a pride in the crisp well-ironed bows on her hair. Black and navy were the usual colours and for additional uplift there was wire-edged ribbon. These bows prevailed until bobbed hair came in, heralded by dancer Irene Castle in 1913 but not generally established until the later stages of the war. With her short (for the time) skirts, general sprightliness in her attire and her big bows, the flapper was the first exponent of the teenage fashions which were to dominate the scene a generation later.

The name flapper is attributed by some to those big bows, which 'flapped'. Others claim that the word was a term originally used for a young duck which, unable to fly properly, was known among wild fowlers as a flapper. The human flapper was symbolically trying her wings in life, and, to strengthen the association of ideas, was at the time often endearingly referred to as a 'duck'. Whichever origin is correct, the facts are that the big bows, the twinkling legs and ankles, the new gaiety, confidence and youthful fun were all bound up with the name and marked a step forward for youth in the social scene. She created a sensation and enjoyed shocking her elders.

In her early days, Miss Drennan recalled, the flapper was recorded in innumerable cartoons and magazine pictures and appeared as a stage character. *Pearson's Magazine* showed her in illustrations by Baliol Salmon to stories by Selwyn Jepson. A flapper called Joy Chatterton was a cartoon character in the *Daily Mirror*. The 17-year-old Evelyn Laye played the flapper rôle of Madeline Manners, in *Going Up* at the Gaiety in May 1918, when she herself was a flapper. *Punch* produced a famous illustrated alphabet during World War I in which 'F was the Flapper who hoped to assist. And told Winston Churchill he ought to enlist', as was recalled in the *Telegraph* by Commander V.F. Smith. This, he explained, was a reference to the reputation flappers had for expressing their patriotism by giving white feathers to any men they found not in uniform.

When, in the 1920s, all skirts were short, all fashions young in style and short hair generally in vogue, there was nothing left to distinguish the flapper from the adult woman and even the dancing grandmother, but the word continued to be used to some degree. It could perhaps be argued that the flapper eventually vanished in a surfeit of success, having conquered all fashion.

The habit of describing children as 'kids' ought to date from somewhere around the flapper age; it conveys the same new note of lightheartedness and camaraderie in its attitude to the young and of distinctiveness in clothing. But though its general use dates from after the start of this century, rising from slang to ordinary speech, its history goes far back. A character in a Massinger play of 1599 says: 'I am old, you say. Yes, parlous old, kids'. In 1690 D'Urfey refers to 'A kid that cry'd'. In 1841 Lord Shaftesbury wrote in his journal: 'Passed a few days happily with my wife and kids'. Ten years later William Morris wrote in a letter: 'Janey and kid are both very well' and the writer Mrs Lynn Linton wrote in 1894: 'The poor kid must have gone to the work-house.' The word 'kiddy' is more recent, with one of its earliest recorded mentions in Kipling's *Barrack Room Ballads* (1892): 'little kiddies sit an' shiver in the carts'. Both words, incidentally, nicely follow the tenets of the 1976 Sex Discrimination Act; all kids and kiddies are equal, free from sex distinction.

Kids' clothes, from about the second decade of this century, meant something new; a carefree, gay, comfortable way of dressing that was to affect all fashion. It was also to bring in new kinds of garments. The first of these was probably rompers, which appeared in the *Oxford English Dictionery*'s 1933 Supplement for the first time as a 'garment for child at play, also (U.S.) style of knickerbockers for men.' The first reference is in the *Westminster Gazette* in 1922, 'an attractive romper suit for a small child is made of white washing material.' The word occurs in *Scribner's* in 1925, while an American writer in 1928 referred to 'very long, very baggy knickers, Hollywood rompers.' The garments, however, seem to go much further back, in style if not in name. In 1865 George Du Maurier, in a letter to his mother written on the first birthday of his daughter Tricksy, said: 'First I must tell you that Tricksy walked unaided across the nursery on her birthday, and it was a great treat to see her; she wears a huge pair of knickerbockers over her petticoats to keep them clean and her appearance is very comical; I wish you could see her.' (Incidentally, he also says in other letters: 'We have been talking about you and the kids.')

The kid in rompers was the new version of the child which came to the fore after the 1914–18 war, that world-wide upheaval and holocaust whose aftermath of social change extended not least to children, though in fact, as has been mentioned, children's clothes in some ways anticipated the changes in those of adults.

July 6—18 only   **The Children's Shop, 352—4, Oxford Street**   July 6—18 only

F1. Coloured Linen Frock, stripe collar and cuffs, suitable for school wear, for ages 6-10 years.

     Sale price 21/-

F2. Lime Serge Costume, trimmed with black Panne velvet.

     Sale price 73/6

F3. Flowered Voile Frock, trimmed lace insertions and ribbon sash. For all ages.

     Sale price 29/6

F4. Figured Voile Frock, with white lawn collar and cuffs, suitable for girls 14-16 years.

     Sale price 42/-

F5. White Embroidered Voile Frock, with tunic and coloured ribbon sash.

     Sale price 63/-

Marshall-grade Bargains in Mackintoshes, Jersey Coats, Millinery (greatly reduced), Jersey Suits, Linen and Cotton Frocks, Woven Combinations, Summer Costumes, Boys' Suits in linen and material.

The Children's Sale lasts a Fortnight Only

92   'Children' of 1914 and their fashions, as seen in a Marshall and Snelgrove sale catalogue

11 Greater Freedom and American Influences

World War I was a watershed in children's dress even more so than in that of adults. 'The 1914 war had an enormous effect on children's clothes', said Pearl Binder in *Muffs and Morals* (1953). 'They went into the war in black cashmere stockings and dressed as stiffly as their mothers and fathers. They emerged in loose and easy clothes, with bobbed hair, jerseys, soft collars, socks instead of stockings. And since then there has been no looking back.'

The changes started with infants. They too lost the last of their shackles. By the end of the war long clothes had been reduced to at most 27 inches and were worn for only the first month or two. By 1930 they had shrunk to 24 inches. The layette of layers of garments that had nearly smothered generations of infants had at last dwindled to a vest, petticoat and dress, with a knitted matinée jacket for cool days and simple coats for out-of-doors after the brief shawl stage. Bonnets were still worn at times, but they too tended to disappear as the fetish of the covered head was abandoned generally. Designs of clothes were simple and basic, with frills and lace largely limited to christening robes and special occasion garments. Simple knitted bootees and mitts covered feet and hands. Bibs worn at the neck were allowed a certain amount of ornamentation for the very young.

Up to the 1930s boys as well as girls wore dresses in their first months, but they were simple, short smocks, usually with matching pants, bloomer-style and very practical for the toddler. Plain knitted leggingettes and jackets and matching cloth leggingettes and coats were other practical twosomes for the toddler and small child. Little boys wore updated versions of the skeleton suit – brief shorts buttoning on to a simple shirt top, often in matching checked and plain Viyella or other practical materials.

Girls wore simple yoked or straight dresses in their early years and other early garments were the same for both sexes. Both alike went into jerseys at an early stage, and party clothes were simple. Silk and crepe de Chine for the tinies, with velvet dresses, or shorts with silk shirts, for winter festivities. With the arrival of man-made fibres in the mid-twenties pretty rayon materials were much used for children's wear, and nursery prints were produced specially for the young market.

Ankle-length socks, usually white, became general at this time, extending from small children to older girls and then, in colours and white, being adopted by women for golf and tennis, over stockings to start with. By the mid-thirties,

93 Dressed for best in 1919 in a natural shantung coat, leghorn straw hat, trimmed with shaded blue periwinkles, pleated tulle underbrim and ties

94   Simple, easy fashions for
children continued with little
change through the 1920s and
1930s. Smocks, rompers, Buster
suits and jerseys were worn
everywhere, as in this Chilprufe
catalogue of 1934

however, women were wearing them bare-legged, like children, for tennis. This fashion was seen for the first time in tournament play at Forest Hills in 1931, the sponsor being the elegant Mrs Eileen Fearnley-Whittingstall.

During World War I girls were wearing straight, extremely short, dresses with hip-line belts and skirts that were no more than a frill below them. A 1915 *Punch* advertisement shows one of them complete with the huge ribbon bow in her hair which was by then becoming popular with all ages of girl and not just the teenage 'flapper'. School uniforms followed fashion so far as they could, thus breaking away from their original endeavour to escape from it to something more rational. A description of a 1921–2 uniform, recalled by the wearer much later, says that 'tunics were as short as possible and girdles as low as possible' – in accordance with adult fashions only just coming in at the time and at last free from restrictions and disarmingly simple, even childish.

Children went along with adults in another fashion of the immediate post-war years – and of all years since then. This was the wearing of hand-knitted jumpers and pullovers, cardigans, scarves and caps by both boys and girls. It was a spin-off from the universal zeal for knitting 'comforts' for the troops during the war – a zeal which extended from grandmothers to school-girls and which seems extraordinarily odd in retrospect. Why should it have been left to private enterprise and money to contribute to the clothing of

95   Girls of 1919, as shown in a Harrods catalogue

96   The schoolboy of the 1920s
and later

soldiers and sailors fighting for their country? It was so, however, and it started a fashion for hand-knitting which has lasted ever since and has affected everyone's clothing.

Schoolboys had gone into flannel shorts or trousers, with blazers, for general wear before men adopted flannel slacks for informal and leisure occasions after the 1914 war. It was among very young men that the first startling male fashion for about a century appeared in 1919 in the shape – or shapelessness – of the very voluminous trousers known as 'Oxford bags', which rapidly swept into fashion among students and other young men. One measurement gives 25 inches round the knees and 22 inches at the bottom of the legs. They were worn everywhere, including America, taken from England by vacationing students. In 1925 John Wannamaker introduced them into his New York store with a full page newspaper advertisement of them as 'originated by the students of Oxford' and made in Oxford as an assurance of authenticity.

Apart from these specifically youth-inspired contributions to fashion, the immediate post-war years saw quite a 'youth explosion' affecting a wide area of daily life and therefore of dress. It did not have the force or social impact of the more recent 'explosion' of the 1950s and 1960s, but in its context in time it was remarkable enough as the first real challenge to the domination of the older generation. With the end of the ironically named 'war to end war' the young leapt into a round of the gaiety of which they had for so long been deprived – a gaiety compounded of jazz, frenetic dances, Noël Coward songs, 'Bright Young things', all elements linked by being dedicated to youth. Young fashions dominated the scene, and the straight short dresses of smart women were almost identical with those of little girls. Ankle-strap shoes were another childish fashion adopted by adults, and sandals also rose from the nursery to reign as a general fashion which has lasted from that day to this.

The huge social upheaval which the 1914–18 war had caused was quick to affect children because it greatly changed the attitudes of parents to the young. From the wreckage of war and its toll of life unequalled in any past conflict people had to look to the future and the new generation for their hopes for a better world. It was an age of psycho-analysis, of child psychology, of the popularity of Freud and the tracing of later psychological defects and troubles to a misunderstood childhood. There was a widespread fear among thoughtful and progressive parents that children would suffer from repressions, inhibitions and complexes if thwarted by severe discipline in their early years. There was a vogue for schools which rejected the traditional regimentation and disciplines and advocated all-out freedom for the young however violent its forms and however destructive its effects. New concepts of education were put into practice as never before, mostly aimed at encouraging self-expression and giving rein to individuality.

Spearheading the movement was headmaster A.S. Neill, advocating complete equality between pupils and teachers, entire abolition of the generation gap and freedom for children to choose how, when and what they should be taught at their schools. His own school, Summerhill, founded in 1924, was a constant sensation in the 1920s and 1930s. It has now passed its half-century at Leiston, Suffolk. His methods and his series of *Dominie* books on education had more influence in America than in Britain, his main inspiration being the American educationalist Homer Lane. 'A few millions, mostly in the U.S.A. and Germany, have read one or two of my books. Many schools in the U.S.A. have been inspired by Summerhill', he says in his autobiography, published in 1972 in America and in 1973 in Britain. It goes without saying that he was anti-uniforms: 'I have always been unconventional about dress and behaviour.'

The *Dominie* books appeared between 1915 and 1924. They contributed in no small measure to the child's charter of rights which today is widely accepted in many of its facets and which has done much to change attitudes about children's education – and children's fashions.

Most of the trends of the 1920s and 1930s were, however, not wholly or even mainly a children's movement, but were closely linked to a new general outlook and to widespread social changes in which children's inclusion was a measure of their newly admitted importance. This was particularly true of the cult for fresh air, sunshine and, for the first time, sunbathing. The important thing was that children were embraced by them all – and as children, not miniature adults.

The sun cult, the idea of sunbathing, of exposing the body to the sun and glorying in becoming sunburnt was entirely new. It began in California, Miami, Florida and other American sun spots in the 1920s. By the latter part of that decade it had spread to the Riviera, 'discovered' as a rapidly growing summer resort of fashion instead of being only the winter retreat of Royalty and other privileged people escaping from the rigours of the British fogs and ice. Americans, many of them already linked with Europe by marriage into the British aristocracy, were to the fore in popularizing Riviera resorts and American-inspired play-clothes, something quite new to fashion, accompanied them. They were usually exiguous, exposing most of the body to the sun. Playsuits, often very like children's rompers and inspired by them, became part of the feminine wardrobe. Men took to shorts, which up to then had been limited to their young sons, to dwellers in the tropics and to footballers and scoutmasters, none of whom would claim to be fashion leaders. Film star Al Jolson is credited with having been the first to have appeared in shorts, khaki-coloured, at the Los Angeles Country Club about 1929. Women, too, rapidly began wearing shorts for holidays, sport, cycling and the popular hiking, and small girls were miniatures of their elders. American tennis star Alice Marble of San Francisco appeared in shorts at a tennis tournament in 1933, to be closely followed by British leaders in a game that was then at the height of its popularity. Shorts became accepted games kit at girls' schools – and they got shorter and shorter.

It took this adult sun cult to get children finally released from the covered-up look. By the 1930s from infancy onwards they were wearing minimal seaside and hot-weather clothes. Brown babies disported themselves on the beach, in gardens and parks. Little sun-suits were part of the summer wardrobe of the young from their earliest days and for the first time ever in civilized society children went down to the sea in slips – the briefs in which they have met summer sun ever since.

Interest in sports and games grew, fostered by the rise in air travel and

97   Working-class school-
children, 1924

motoring. Out of doors activities came within the reach of the many instead
of only the few. It might almost be said that adults were behaving like children
in their love of games and in the clothes they wore for them, instead of requiring that children should be small adults, as in the past.

Blue-jeans are so much part of the children's clothes scene that they cannot
be omitted from it, even though they belong to the strange new revival of the
old-time picture of children as miniature adults. Though jeans have had their
heyday from the 1950s until the present time, they too came into young
fashion in those sartorially significant between-the-wars years. The first
wearers of them in this context were students of the University of California,
who took to them in the 1930s and thereby started a world-wide, all-ages, all-
classes fashion which has become almost a way of life.

The jeans and bright shirts, which today's child wears so proudly, were
originally the attire of American slaves and later of the coloured working
population. Their rise into fashion came with the craze for jazz, which started
among the coloured people of America, the original Dixieland Jazz band
being formed in 1916 in New Orleans. From there it went to New York and
Chicago and then to London. It gave great prestige to the coloured American
population, making their clothes fashionable. The return of colour to male
clothes, adult and juvenile, derives largely from this long concatenation.

Jean, a stout twilled cotton, originated in Genoa, whence it acquired its
name, and was used for clothes for men, women and children from the
eighteenth century. Eton cricketers in 1820 wore 'a white jean jacket fitting
closely to the figure', according to the college historian, H.C. Maxwell Lyte.
Jean was, however, used mainly for work clothes until its modern vogue began
and blue was traditionally the usual colour, due to the cheapness of the dye.

A further boost for jeans came from their also being worn by cowboys of the American West who had become a picturesque feature of life there after the Civil War settled the country. Cowboys were later seized upon as subjects of the 'Westerns' which were a dominating feature of the cinema and a major part of the entertainment world from the 1920s. 'Westerns' were the particular joy of boys of all ages from then to this day and cowboy outfits became the delight of youngsters.

Denims, as popular with the young as jeans, also have a long history although their main vogue in fashion also dates from the past twenty years. They originated in 1850, when Levi Strauss, a gold prospector, went to California and had the idea of making work pants of indigo blue denim, reinforced with copper rivets at points of stress. He made a bigger fortune from them than would probably have come to him from the often elusive gold, and he also laid the foundations of a fashion revolution headed by the young of a century later. 'Levis' are today a household word, with Junior Levis as a sub-division, and they still have the label introduced in 1873.

The Old World, however, made one contribution of its own which influenced boys' fashions in the 1930s. Corduroys, traditionally worn by the British working man and farm labourer, became highly popular with young boys in the 1930s and, both as shorts and as the greatly coveted 'longs', to which youngsters aspired at an early age, corduroys attained the sacrosanct heights of accepted school uniform. Among adults, corduroys had earlier found favour with artists, who saw in them a symbol of revolt against the conventions of middle and upper class dress. Needless to say, the elevation of corduroys among the great middle classes did not promote them to a higher status among their original wearers. No workman would have dreamed of wearing them except for their original purpose.

While all these democratic, mainly transatlantic influences were being brought to bear on children's fashions the long reign of Royal children as fashion leaders entered what was to be its final phase in the 1930s, when Princess Elizabeth and Princess Margaret became the models for the dress followed by mothers all over the country for their small daughters. The 'Rosebud dress', embroidered with posies of that flower on collar, sleeves and pockets, was copied widely in the early 1930s from a style worn by Princess Elizabeth. In 1932, when Princess Margaret was two, the 'Margaret Rose' frock, faithfully copied and given the name by which she was then known, won first prize in a knitting competition run by a well-known women's magazine. The little princesses also wore pleated skirts and woollen jerseys, just like any other small girls. The smocks worn by the young Duke of Kent, born in 1935, were also adopted for innumerable small boys of similar age everywhere. In 1937, when Princess Elizabeth was 11, *Wife and Home* declared to its readers: 'Mothers are looking to your young Princesses to set the fashion in children's wear this season, and they will heartily approve the simple styles chosen by the Queen for her little daughters.' These included practical holiday jerseys and double-breasted tailored coats – clothes that were already being worn by children everywhere. Royal dress had become thoroughly democratic as it bowed itself out as a model for other children. It had already ceased to be a trend-setter for adults, the last Royal fashion-setter having been the princesses' great-grandmother, Queen Alexandra. Later both princesses wore

98   Princess Elizabeth and Princess Margaret in simple tailored coats when they attended the Royal Tournament in 1935 with the Queen, now Queen Elizabeth the Queen Mother

the uniforms of Girl Guide and Brownie respectively, when they became part of a Buckingham Palace pack formed in 1937. It was a far cry from the past spectacle of Royal children decked out as miniature field marshals and generals, of princesses in ruffs and farthingales in the style of their mothers, and even of the Highland dress and sailor outfits of boys and girls of the previous century. Children were now allowed to be children everywhere. The Duke of Kent and his sister, Princess Alexandra, were even photographed later in dungarees, about 1950.

The cult of the child found expression in the 1930s in a mass adulation that is without parallel in history. It was the world-wide fame of Shirley Temple, the child film-star. The cinema dominated the entertainment world of these days as neither it nor any other medium had ever done, and Shirley Temple dominated the cinema. Mothers all over the world modelled their children on her and her clothes were copied for millions of children and were mass-manufactured everywhere. Her curls, too, set youthful hair styles all over the world.

Born in 1928, she was first discovered by Charles Lamond of Educational Pictures at the age of three and a half, when he was looking for children to appear in *Baby Burlesks*, a series of one-reelers in which she first appeared guying Dolores del Rio and Marlene Dietrich at a starting salary of ten dollars a day. She was then seized upon by Fox Films and in 1934 made the first of an astonishing series of successful films, *Stand Up and Sing*, wearing a red and white polka-dot dress which became universally known as the Shirley Temple dress and became a mass fashion – the first ever to be created by a child for children. From the ages of seven to ten (pretended by her parents and studios to be six to nine), she was box office queen of the world; the youngest person ever to appear on the cover of *Time* magazine; the youngest to be included in *Who's Who*; the youngest Academy award winner. She was the only film star ever to top the *Motion Picture Herald's* box office poll for four years running, from 1935 to 1938. She received an Oscar in 1935 as 'the one great towering figure in the cinema game in 1934' and because she 'brought more happiness to millions of children and millions of grown-ups than any child of her years in the history of the world.' By 1935 she was earning 4000 dollars a week and 'under product tie-up deals with ten firms for Shirley Temple dolls, and underwear, coats, hats, shoes, books, hair ribbons, soap, dresses, toys, cereal bowls and milk pitchers she received another 1000 dollars a week', says her latest biographer, Robert Windeler.

99 Shirley Temple set fashions for millions of children all over the world in the 1930s and this dress was copied everywhere

She was said by President Roosevelt, whom she visited at Washington, to have done more than any other person to beat the depression of the 1930s. Her songs became top hits, outselling those of Bing Crosby, Nelson Eddy and other adult stars. Between her fifth and twelfth birthdays she earned more than two million dollars. In 1938 her income was the seventh highest in the U.S.A., the other six being those of leading industrialists. She retired at 12, made a come-back with only limited success as a teenager but ended her film career at 21 with between three and four million dollars untouched. In brief, as summed up by Mr Windeler, 'she was without possibility of argument, the most famous child in the world . . . although she never made a single motion picture that she or anybody else thought was really any good.'

None of her films is seen nowadays. About 75 of her dresses, including some film ones, were sold during World War II by United National Clothing Collection as what she called 'my first adult good deed' at the age of 17. In 1975 I.T.V. considered reviving some of her films for use in children's hour programmes, but decided that they had 'no relevance to modern children. . . . We felt they were just too sentimental and mawkish to interest today's sophisticated children. . . . Her films are more likely to appeal to the nostalgia of older people.' To some perhaps; others, even in the 1930s, avoided them like the plague.

The vogue she enjoyed was fantastic, inexplicable, but it must have had something to do with the way people were looking at their children. As a landmark in the story of children she remains unique. No other child actors have come near her in their impact or had any effect on children's clothes,

though adult film stars of the 1930s influenced women's fashions quite considerably. Deanna Durbin, Bobby Green, Gloria Jean, Mickey Rooney,
Beverley Sills, Jane Withers, Judy Garland, Hayley Mills, Tatum O'Neal,
however dazzling their youthful and subsequent careers, have left no mark
on children's dress. And none of them has, like today's Shirley Temple Black,
become director of several companies, candidate for Congress in 1967, the
only woman delegate to the United Nations in 1970, lecturer on ecology,
U.S. ambassador to Ghana – an appointment made by Dr Henry Kissinger in
1974. To crown all, in 1976 she became America's Chief of Protocol, the first
woman to hold that office. From the child-star setting juvenile fashions and
piping out *Animal Crackers in my Soup* to the announcement of 'Shirley
Temple's White House job' is a startling progression even in the startling
world of children's costume.

It was no accident that from the 1920s the influence of America on children's
Apart from Shirley Temple, the only contribution made by the cinema to
children's dress in the period between the wars came from the cartoon makers
and were comparatively minor ones. The first Disney cartoons were made in
the 1920s, with Mickey Mouse dating from about 1928, closely followed by
Donald Duck, then Snow White, his first feature film, in 1937. They were
evidence of the importance being attached to children's entertainment, and
though they did not set fashions they started the vogue for pictorial motifs on
children's garments and nursery equipment. Mickey Mouse and Donald Duck
appeared on millions of nursery feeders and then on T-shirts and other
youthful garments, and also were used as designs for printed fabrics for
children's clothes. *Pinocchio* in 1940, *Dumbo* in 1941 and *Bambi* in 1942 also
testified to the new importance of the child and all these figures pervaded the
nursery as toys, pictures, decorations and as motifs on clothes. The 'fun'
clothes which were to spread to teenagers and young adults in the 1960s
probably had their start in the pre-war and wartime nurseries. They also
marked a new development in the story of children's clothes, from which
'fun' had been conspicuously absent throughout history. Walt Disney did
more than anyone to start it, in real life and to some degree, in dress. When
he died in 1966 he had won over 50 Academy awards and made thousands of
films, most of them for children. They included, between 1928 and 1949,
over 120 Mickey Mouse films, nearly 100 Silly Symphonies, nearly 90 Donald
Duck cartoons, 40 Pluto, 25 Goofy and a large number of full-length features
and short cartoons. Unlike Shirley Temple, he remains as popular today as
he was 40 years ago.

It was no accident that from the 1920s the influence of America on children's
fashions, as on all fashion, grew steadily. The main reason for the general
trend was the lead taken by America in the mass production of clothing
which developed greatly at this time – a lead due mainly to the fact the great
size of the market gave a spur to large-scale manufacture. Ready-to-wear
clothes, which meant simple, moderately-priced and therefore near-classless
clothes, came to the fore of fashion just when fashion was ceasing to be the
monopoly of the wealthy and the aristocratic in a world where class distinctions were becoming blurred.

In this trend American children were ahead of their contemporaries in
Britain because children had always been given more consideration in the

New World than in the Old. This in turn was at least partly due to the fact that the status of women was higher in the former and, as the main custodians of children in day-to-day affairs, women who enjoy power ensure that children are given consideration. Women played an important part among the early American settlers when, with a shortage of labour, their work was indispensable. In the eighteenth and nineteenth century frontier and national wars, as well as in the continuing hazards of pioneer life, women had a degree of equality unknown in the more highly stratified society of western Europe. They served as soldiers, spies and nurses in the Wars of Independence. They got the vote in Wyoming in 1869 and by 1890 four western states had full women's suffrage and several others a limited suffrage. The prominence of Quakers in America also helped the status of women, because Quakers traditionally maintained sex equality in all activities. The effect of all this included not only the assertive American woman but the equally assertive and, to some, the alarmingly self-confident American child.

12 Clothing by Decree: World War II

When in 1930, James Laver wrote that 'children's fashions react more quickly to outside influences than those of their elders. That is their value, as a channel through which modifications can enter', the thought was true for his time. His illustration of it was the great vogue for sailor dress among English and German boys in the pre-1914 period of fierce naval competition between the two Powers concerned. A useful comment on children's dress and perhaps a reason for the prolonged vogue for the fashion among boys – and girls – but not very apt as it did not extend to adults. He was also reflecting his day in still seeing children's fashions as subsidiary to the mainstream of fashion and not a category of their own, as they were to become. In his context he was not concerned with the wider social implications of his statement – with the fact that the vulnerability of the child, the ultimate powerlessness underlying all that enormous impulsive energy and vitality mean that in his clothes, as elsewhere, the child is wide open to adult domination unless adults make the mental and imaginative effort to get on to his wave-length. Few had done so in the past. Outside influences have been imposed on the child to a degree unknown to the adult. The history of children's fashions is therefore bound up with social history in great detail and, conversely, can itself throw light on that social history.

When World War II broke out in September 1939 children's lives, and probably their clothes, were among the first to be subject to the destructive outside influences suddenly released on a massive scale on to daily life – influences not, however, due to be modified later as James Laver might have expected. The evacuation of millions of British children from the supposed perils of cities to the supposed safety of the countryside was a major upheaval, aggravated by being followed by a series of considerable reversals of the process for the same purpose; the famous 'bomb alley' by which German raiders made their way to London across the Kent and Sussex coast was a chosen safety zone favoured by many schools and away-from-it-all remote Caithness got Britain's first bombs when Scapa was attacked by the Luftwaffe. There was a disruption of civilian life such as had never previously been suffered by the British, at any rate in our era. For hundreds of thousands of children it was traumatic, with their whole background swept away overnight on 1 September 1939. That their fashions went into disarray was a minor part of it, but it happened in many cases. It would not be easy or very useful to trace the sartorial fall of the child evacuee, but he must have been the first to feel the wartime clothes stringencies and confusion that were to follow and to last for years, much longer than the war.

This, however, was only the start of the wartime clothes story. This war saw, for the first time in recorded history, fashion and clothing by decree. Clothes rationing, shaped mainly by Ernest Bevin in Churchill's coalition government, was introduced in June 1941 in face of Churchill's initial violent opposition to it. The announcement was made by Capt. Oliver Lyttleton, President of the Board of Trade and later the first Lord Chandos, in a broadcast on 1 June and rationing began on 7 June. The allocation was 66 coupons per person for 12 months and the scheme started with the curious arrangement that 'until special cards are available, 26 margarine coupons in the current Food Ration book will be used for clothing.' After a week Churchill admitted that Lyttleton was right, but, initially at least, the move was counter-inflationary rather than practically necessary, part of Maynard Keynes' economic policy.

Coupons had to be given up in fixed numbers for almost everything worn Children were recognized as a separate category from the start, with special concessions made then and later to allow for the problems of growing out of clothes. From the start clothing coupons were interchangeable between husband, wife and children, but not otherwise. In the men's and boys' categories of coupon values of garments those of boys were in almost all cases

100　The evacuation of children to safety areas in 1939 was a major upheaval which affected their whole way of life – and their clothes

lower than those of men, with only minor exceptions like accessories – collars, ties, handkerchiefs, scarves, gloves and, oddly, corduroys. Similarly, girls' clothes were rated lower than those of women. Special consideration was from the start given to growing children in the shape of the concession that children too big for the official children's sizes would receive extra coupons, which would also be available for wool for knitting garments for babies. Infants up to four were originally exempt from rationing, as was certain industrial clothing.

Amendments quickly followed the introduction of clothes rationing, mostly affecting children. Thus, on 5 July extra coupons were allowed for expectant mothers, and 66, through the Children's Overseas Reception Board, to parents of children evacuated overseas; an odd concession as British wartime clothes would not be likely to enhance the American or Canadian scene and it would surely have been simpler to allow money to be sent. People bombed out and losing their possessions, were given one year's extra coupons – nothing like enough to equip adult or child.

In August 1941 babies' clothing was rationed, those born between then and 30 November receiving 40 coupons and those between December and May 30 coupons, plus 50 for knitting wool for mothers. It was pointed out by one writer that though you would not start your life without clothing coupons you could leave it couponless – shrouds were not included in clothes rationing.

In November 1941 it became legal for second-hand school clothing to be sold by licensed traders without coupons to pupils of the same school. On the next day the Board of Education instructed school authorities and governing bodies to rescind from 20 December 1941 regulations requiring school uniforms to be worn – but many did not do so and school uniforms often became an acute family problem. When, in March 1942 clothing coupons were reduced by 25 per cent and their validity extended to 14 months, ten supplementary coupons were given to children under 17.

Much more drastic in many ways than rationing of clothes was the Utility scheme, announced in March 1942 by Hugh Dalton, who had taken over as President of the Board of Trade. Aimed at saving work and cloth, it meant that for nearly ten years government rules and regulations controlled the substance, shape and design of almost everything that everybody wore, regardless of age, rank and wealth or poverty. Regulations specified the nature, quality and amount of materials used for clothes and the price to be charged for every item. The design of clothes was controlled. At first the scheme applied to 50 per cent of all production but later, as materials and labour both became scarcer, this was raised to 85 per cent. Though the remaining 'free' area of clothing was unrestricted in the price and the nature of materials, made-up clothing was universally controlled by restrictions on style and amount of materials.

In ancient Greece and Rome and in the Middle Ages in various countries there had been sumptuary laws forbidding the wearing of certain clothes and certain colours by those below a certain rank, but never had there been a system embracing every person in this way. The Utility scheme began to show its teeth in 1942, especially in regard to men's and boys' clothing. From

1 May jackets could no longer be double-breasted, could not have more than three pockets, none of them patch in style, could not have slits or buttons on cuffs, could not have belts or more than three front buttons, which must not be of metal or leather. Trousers could not have turn-ups, could not be more than 19 inches at the bottom of the leg. They were not allowed pleats, elastic, rubber or fabric waistbands or belts or zip fastenings. Waistcoats were similarly restricted. From April men's and boys' shirts had to be shorter, to save material, and double cuffs and double fronts were banned. Pyjamas could not have pockets or trimmings.

For girls and women coats could not have capes or trimmings of fur, silk, rayon or leather. Trimmings of beads, embroidery, braid and everything else were forbidden. Skirts could not have more than 6 seams, one pocket, two box pleats or four knife pleats. No flares or all-round pleats were permitted. No trimming was allowed on underwear or nightwear and the amount of material and even the width of hems were both limited. From June 1942 even the Utility baby was not allowed to have embroidery or trimmings on his clothes. His pockets and buttons were also rationed.

In August 1943, Hugh Dalton announced an extension of the extra 10 or 20 coupons for growing children to those born between 1924 and 1926 or reaching the height of 5ft 3in or weight of 7st 12lbs by October 1942. In spite of concessions, however, children were among the worst sufferers from clothes rationing and, even more, from the rigours of the Utility scheme. Up to the age of 11 or 12 boys had no choice but shorts and being deprived of the 'longs', which by this time were much coveted, was a particular grievance. Children's shoes were much harder to find than those of adults. With the fall of Malay rubber became scarce and school-children's plimsolls disappeared, to the great annoyance of games enthusiasts. So did Wellington boots, another bulwark of the young wardrobe. Though the Utility scheme was in many ways rated as his big success, Hugh Dalton later said in his memoirs that he believed that public indignation about children's clothes may have cost him votes in the 1945 General Election.

In general, however, the Utility scheme was not so utterly depressing as it sounds in today's context of extreme permissiveness. In fact it was even beneficial. Utility regulations were worked out with the cooperation of top fashion designers and, as was seen afterwards, they did much to rationalize clothing manufacture and to make the fashion trade, notoriously ill-organized, put its house in order. By encouraging straightforward design and eliminating fussy trimmings the Utility scheme probably in the end benefited children most of all, simplifying their clothes and, in particular, stopping doting mothers from dressing up toddlers and small girls like fruit-cakes, with frills and flounces, buttons and bows, all aimed at showing off parental prosperity and success rather than benefiting the wearers.

The struggle to clothe a growing family was, however, acute, and rationing outlasted the war. In the immediate post-war years a holiday in Eire, where clothes rationing was unknown, was often the only opportunity to equip a child satisfactorily. He or she would cross the Irish channel with almost nothing except what was worn and return with a complete wardrobe, well-styled and in good materials. From America the 'Bundles for Britain' scheme,

101   Clothes like this, familiar today, dated from the American influence exerted during World War II. A snow suit by Kamella

whereby American families collected clothing as for a kind of super jumble sale and sent it across the Atlantic for the destitute British, initially for the bombed-out, then for others too, produced an almost unbelievable range of new-style children's clothes which, in the view of Iris Brooke, was the start of the post-war revolution in children's clothes and especially the rise of 'casuals'. 'It was' she says, 'all part of the "Costume" of war years to find small boys in loudly checked or plaid three-quarter length coats with belts, brightly coloured knitted caps and the strangest ankle boots with toe caps and low lacing. The smallest child was to be seen wearing long trousers and knee breeches with elastic at the knee, and snow-suits hitherto unknown in England were everywhere to be seen worn by girls and boys indiscriminately. So thick and cosy were these useful garments that conventional children's clothes in England practically disappeared in favour of the much-prized "Yank" possessions.' The 'urchin cut' for hair in 1948, shirts worn outside trousers, rolled-up slacks were all, she adds, wartime and post-war fashions for children which came from the U.S.A.

When America came into the war in December 1941 life there became less easy and subsequently some clothes rationing was introduced, but to a small extent compared with Britain. There the restrictions continued until years after the war, so that millions of children spent their formative years with no knowledge of anything except clothes dominated by rules and regulations. Some easing, however, was introduced. In May 1946 Sir Stafford Cripps, then President of the Board of Trade, announced the removal of nearly all austerity clothing and footwear restrictions, which meant that trimmings, embroidery, pleats, buttons and so forth were allowed on women's, girls' and children's clothes, while men's suits got back their pockets, trouser turn-ups and other embellishments. In 1948, Harold Wilson, then at the Board of Trade, announced that children's footwear was to be coupon-free. On 14 March 1949 he 'announced the complete abolition of the rationing of clothes and of all forms of textiles as from March 15.' The Utility scheme, he added, would go on and even be increased in certain areas of clothing. Rationing had lasted for nearly eight years. The Utility scheme, in a somewhat liberated form, was to continue until 1952.

It is an indication of America's comparative detachment from wartime clothes privations that in the early 1940s that country gave recognition to a new pre-teen age-group of children by naming them 'bobbysoxers', a word that became part of the English language. The distinguishing mark of this group was the short ankle-length socks they wore. The word was used in *The Times* in 1943 and was generally current in the U.S.A. where in 1944 a horde of bobbysoxers hit the headlines by getting so out of control that the police had to be called in to restore order. The word became common in the later 1940s and 1950s, but is out of date today. In the 1950s the grown-up Shirley Temple admitted she was behind the fashion in sending her young daughter to school in what had become a despised style of leg covering. The reality of the disruptive young mob of 1944, is, however, still very much with us in the scenes of mass teenage hysteria over the 'pop' heroes of today at airports and concert halls, as their fans besiege them.

Somewhat surprising, in face of Britain's wartime restrictions and shortages, was the tenacity with which school uniforms were retained. The cynical might say that all clothing was uniform anyway, but that did not answer the problem of special outfits. Many school heads argued that uniforms contributed to morale and the stiff-upper-lipped among them were particularly insistent, in spite of Oliver Lyttleton having freed them from the need to maintain this tradition of the private sector of education. There was also the argument that uniforms were a practical way of expending clothes coupons because they curbed the impulse to seek a wide variety of clothing which might have been unleashed by freedom of choice.

Such uniforms did, however, become simpler and less formal in most cases. *Junior Age*, the trade paper of the children's clothing manufacturers, said as early as 1940, before clothes rationing was thought of, that 'in most quarters it is believed that the war has sounded the death-knell for blue serge and black suits for boys. They have not been popular with boys for years now . . . Flannel suits, tweed coats and suits are taking their place.' School uniforms were still largely confined to public, grammar and high schools. By 1939 boys at most of these were already in grey flannel or brown or fawn corduroy shorts or long trousers with school blazers. The alternative was the grey flannel suit, still widely worn to this day. The blazer too retains its popularity and is still universally worn by boys and girls at schools of all kinds. A strong stimulus towards the extension of school uniforms was given before the end of the war by Mr R.A., later Lord, Butler's very important 1944 Education Act which extended the leaving age to 15 and then to 16, and provided secondary education for all at grammar, technical or secondary modern schools. Before the war only 14 per cent of children had proceeded beyond elementary schools. Under the new dispensation school uniforms progressively became almost universal. They remain so.

During the war the retention of uniforms was observed mainly in the private sector. Eton retained its suit, though it disappeared finally from its birthplace in the 1950s. The war put an end to the top hat at Eton, for the practical reason that it could not be worn with the gas masks which, by a colossal official misjudgment, were carried for years by the whole populace and regarded as almost a kind of talisman against any kind of disaster. There was, incidentally, a special Mickey Mouse style of gas mask, painted in a cheerful red and blue, for small children, in order to allay their fears. A special hood for infants looked more fearsome than the old-time swaddling bands and was found quite unusable by many mothers. Luckily it never had to be used.

The most traditional school uniforms were the most persistent in face of pleas for austerity, Norman Longmate, in *How We Lived Then*, his account of daily life in wartime Britain, comments: 'The prize for stupidity and selfish indifference to both the national need and common sense must surely go to my own school, which dressed its eight hundred boys in a ridiculous, uncomfortable and unhygienic Tudor ensemble of ankle-length gown, knee breeches, long, thick, yellow stockings and vast but shapeless shirt, without collar or cuffs, . . . though the school did allow new boys to dress normally for their first year or two, the rest of us continued to look as if we were expecting the

102 Smart summer dresses and blazers for girls of the North London Collegiate School in the 1950s

Spanish Armada rather than the German Army, and almost all our coupons were simply appropriated to maintain this famous tradition.' So much for Christ's Hospital.

Among schoolgirls too change had already been on its way by 1939 and the war probably only accelerated the natural course of events. Simpler and more attractive styles of tunics or skirts with blouses or jerseys were taking the place of the famous gym tunic, the original symbol of the Victorian school-girl's liberation from fashion into commonsense. As the gym tunic had never been becoming or had any relation to fashion, the effect of the war and of its sensibly designed Utility clothes was probably good, bringing the young girl's school uniform more in line with current fashion.

So far as feminine fashion was concerned the later 1940s did not repeat the extreme 'young' look of the 1920s which had brought such a close approximation between adult and juvenile styles of dressing after World War I. The famous New Look introduced by Christian Dior in February 1947 did not have any effect on the dress of small girls. With its high bust, tiny waist, full skirt and voluminous petticoats it was a blissful liberation for the war-spent woman weary of shortages and restrictions, but it was nostalgic, with a dying fall, and had nothing for the forward-looking young girl, whose freedom was fully accepted.

Surprisingly, in view of what was to come in the shape of the 'youth explosion', the immediate post-war years produced very few changes in children's and young people's clothes. Boys had blazers, sports jackets, pull-overs, sports shirts, flannels and corduroys, but not jeans or denims or T-shirts. Girls wore orthodox dresses, skirts and blouses or jerseys and often shorts for games. The main change for both lay in the development of man-made fibres and fabrics, which meant that easy-care, drip-dry, non-iron materials brought a revolution to the nursery and schoolroom. Light and pretty clothes did not have to be protected so rigorously from soiling. Boys could be boys with fewer reprimands from mothers over the state of their clothes.

The children's charter for freedom was endorsed by Mrs Margaret Thatcher when, opening the Junior Fashion Fair in 1959, she called for less ugly school-wear, better and more intelligible sizing codes and the production of wash-able, easy-care clothes in every category.

The first sign of changes to come was significant in that it was a prime example of the youthful assertion of the right to choose what to wear, that it was classless – and that it came from America. It was the Davy Crockett 'Western' outfit, and especially the Davy Crockett hat, inspired by the Walt Disney film of 1955, which was shown all round the world and generated a craze for imitation wherever it was shown. The film itself was a freak fashion influence. It was originally made as a three-part TV drama which 'proved so successful that it was released as a feature film and generated a merchandizing bonanza' in Davy Crockett outfits, according to Disney's biographer, Richard Schickel, who adds that it 'started one of the great juvenile fads of the decade.' The tufted fur hat, highly unbecoming, was in enormous demand. In 1956 *The Times* recorded that domestic cats were being killed to supply skins for Davy Crockett hats for children and the same subject led to a protest being made by Lord Scarsdale at a meeting of the R.S.P.C.A.

By the 1950s the post-war rise in the birth-rate was making itself felt in the

103   The Davy Crockett outfit started a fashion that swept the small boy's world of the late 1950s. Here is star of the film, Fess Parker, in the original version

growing proportion of young people reaching the stage of asserting their wants. In America, where this was most pronounced, the number of children between the ages of five and 14 doubled between 1940 and 1965, when one third of all U.S. citizens were under 14. Children were an important market for the clothes trade numerically as well as in the attention being given to them.

In Britain the first recognition of the increasing assertiveness of the young in the clothes world came in a highly surprising form and context. It was the emergence of the Teddy Boy in the late 1940s and 1950s and his rapid development into a frantic cult. Its significance was threefold. First and foremost, his outfit was the first in costume history to be promoted by the young for the young. The Teddy Boy was usually in his mid-teens and was either a schoolboy or in his first job. His outfit was also the first fashion to make its start among the lower classes. The Teddy Boy was essentially working-class and assertively so. Finally, it was the first fashion to be the outward evidence of a life-style, a personality cult, and was not based on upper-class leadership. The Teddy Boy's main *milieu* was the East End of London and the corresponding areas of other cities and was associated with a certain amount of hooliganism. He was also entirely a British phenomenon, with no American or continental affiliations. Nor did he want to rise out of the closed social circle in which he moved. He broke the hitherto unquestioned link of fashion with social aspirations. No adult fashion had yet done this, but he started a trend that was soon to penetrate deeply into fashion as a whole.

The start of the Teddy Boy is generally accepted as deriving from the rather Edwardian look introduced into male fashions by the Dress Council when wartime restrictions were lifted. When the men's and boy's Utility suit was abolished in 1946 it disappeared without regret. In a natural reaction from it there was a vogue for longer, more shapely jackets, with high revers, elaborate cuffs and pocket flaps, for elegant waistcoats and for carefully cut, narrow trousers. The Teddy boy version exaggerated this picture to grotesque extremes, added a number of features that were quite out of context, and stereotyped it. The trousers were drainpipe-narrow and usually black. They were often shortish in the leg, exposing startling socks of bright yellow or orange. The jacket was loose, with extremely wide, padded shoulders, and was very long, almost skirted, often coming below the wearer's thighs, with a conspicuous 'drape' and often an Edwardian velvet collar. A very narrow tie, little more than a string, was worn with a high stiff collar, another Edwardian touch. Several heavy brass or gilt rings might be worn. At first shoes were flat, chunky 'creepers', but by the 1950s they were pointed-toe 'winkle-pickers'. The Teddy Boy wore his hair long, with a quiff in front, perhaps side-burns, and the famous 'DA' or 'duck's arse' cut at the back.

As suited the times and perhaps his context, this freak version of the Edwardian 'masher' had a feminine counterpart, a teenager who went around with him. She wore a black skirt and a tight, black, high-necked sweater, a grey, waisted jacket, coming well down over her hips, fine nylon stockings, usually black, and very high-heeled shoes which in the 1950s became the famous stilettos which also had 'winkle-picker' pointed toes.

Almost forgotten today and in appearance as remote as though he belonged to 200 and not just some 20 years ago, the Teddy Boy had an influence wider

104   Teddy Boys in the 1950s

than his limited ambience suggests. 'In terms of English teenagers', says Nik Cohn in *Today there are no Gentlemen*, 'Teddy Boys were the start of everything; rock 'n roll and coffee bars, clothes and bikes and language, juke boxes and coffee with froth on it – the whole concept of a private teen life style, separate from the adult world.' That this life-style started when it did, he suggests, was due to the fact that for the first time the young had money. The short-lived affluent society had arrived, with well-paid jobs extending to the very young. Before the war middle- and working-class young people had shared most of their activities with their parents through lack of money, just as (one might add) their parents had the main say in what they wore because the parents had the money. This is partly true, but changed adult attitudes had also a lot to do with the start of it. Pocket money for the young was lavish, the permissive society, indulging the young, was on its way and, once started, it went on apace.

105   The Beatles in Washington, 1964

The Teddy Boy cult was succeeded by other similar phenomena, with more and more young people adopting a distinctive style of dress based on this new grouping of the wearers by social and psychological cohesion and not by conventional class distinctions or aspirations. The 1950s were also the era of the 'Mod', given to mohair suits and defined, rather vaguely, by Hamlyn's *Encyclopaedic Dictionary* of 1971 as 'a young person who dresses in ultra-fashionable manner and identifies himself (or herself) with others who affect a similar style of dress.' The Rocker, of the same period, was described by the same source as a 'young person characterized by rough unruly behaviour, who usually wears leather clothing and rides a motor cycle.' The 'ton-up boys' stemmed from this. The ultimate in this trend came in the early 1960s with the Beatles. They made their first big impact in 1962 when they cut their record *Love Me Do*, which swept through the young generation. 'By the summer of 1963', to return to Nik Cohn, 'Beatle-mania was raging at full force and the great teenage boom was under way, a cult that turned Carnaby Street from a backwater into a massive world-wide madness.' Up to then teenage life (and clothes) had been a sporadic, intermittent breakaway from the main trend of adult life. After this, it became an entity in itself, 'Suddenly kids were the focus . . . They became the centre of rapt attention, to be studied and analyzed and aped.'

America is said to have invented the teenager, and attention was being given to this group there before Britain became involved. But Britain took the lead in the development of the cult in most of its aspects. Britain brought the teenager into the mainstream of feminine fashion when Mary Quant launched herself into the fashion world in the 1950s with the design and promotion of clothes that were expressly for the young. 'I had', she said, 'always wanted the young to have fashions of their own . . . absolutely twentieth-century fashions' and as they did not exist she proceeded, starting from scratch, to create them and make them world-famous. By 1962 she and her husband, Alexander Plunket Greene, were 'ultra front room people' to *Vogue*. The 'London Look' became famous and the chief feature of it was the mini-skirt, which she developed with immense *bravura* from 1965, though in fact it was first seen in the revolutionary Paris collection of Courrèges. It was young fashion rampant, not indeed wholly teenage fashion but something conceivable only in a world in which youth was at the prow – as it now was for the first time.

Mary Quant took the mini-skirt triumphantly to America, creating a sensation there and making a major contribution to the Youth Revolution that was sweeping the western world. 'London', she said, 'led the way in changing the focus of fashion from the Establishment to the young. As a country we were aware of the great potential of these clothes long before the Americans or the French.' The heady excitement of 'Swinging London' is ancient history now, but at its time, in the 1960s, it meant the triumph of the young for the first time. By flaunting their own kind of fashions they proclaimed their self-assertion. They led the way for women of all ages to wear shorter skirts, to take to stocking tights, to adopt a way of dressing which expressed a life-style and not the social distinction implicit in the traditional Establishment.

The Youth Revolution was not wholly due to a new great advance in the recognition of the rights of the young, though such recognition had been gaining force, especially in the present century. The plain fact was that the young had suddenly and for the first time become big business for the fashion manufacturer – and for other manufacturers catering for their suddenly important and manifold tastes. In a world of full employment which by the 1950s 'had never had it so good', there were abundant jobs and opportunities for young people. Their wages were high as they had never been before and clothes had a high priority among the items on which their money was spent, especially in the teenage freedom from responsibilities and commitments.

The dress of younger children was to follow that of teenagers, but it moved more slowly. Being economically dependant on their parents the very young were still more affected by adult tastes, though they followed increasingly in the footsteps of their older brothers and sisters where clothes and ways of life were concerned. Janey Ironside has recorded the great difficulties she ran into when, in the 1950s, she turned her energies towards trying to design better clothes for young children and to get such clothes into production. In spite of the support of the *Sunday Express*, *Vogue* and *Queen*, including three pages of pictures of her designs for Horrockses' Pirouette range for children in *Vogue* in April 1955 and more in the following autumn, her bitter conclusion was that 'it was obvious that these clothes were not wanted by the children's wear shops and departments.' Conventional designs, years old, died hard – but die they did, by the 1960s. That went for adult fashions too, but youth had given the lead.

13 Enter the Manufacturing Giants

The over-riding impetus behind the developments in children's fashions in recent years, as in all fashions, came from the continuous rise of ready-to-wear during the past century and, more explicitly, the even more recent and more important development of mass production and large-scale advertising and promotion, both the latter being particularly notable in the children's market, with the new purpose of catching the child's eye and attention, not those of the parent.

These developments have perhaps had more effect on children's fashions than on those of adults but, to go back a long way for a moment, it may well be that on the ready-to-wear side children's fashions can notch up another 'first' in costume history.

Children's clothes, being on the whole simpler and less shaped than those of grown-ups and children themselves usually also being simpler in shape, this area of fashion was a 'natural' for the ready-to-wear market. Children outgrew their clothes and were impatient over fittings, so inexpensive, ready-made garments were very suitable for them. The revolution in clothes production started by the invention of the sewing machine as a practical piece of equipment (Elias Howe's version in 1848, that of Isaac Merrit Singer in 1851, both in America) was felt in the children's market before it seriously affected adult fashions. Still largely confined to the privileged few, the latter were too elaborate for large-scale production. Ready-made was a derogatory word until well into the present century for most of what aspired to the name of fashion in outerwear and, to a considerable degree, in much of women's underwear.

Though the lack of information about early children's clothes is matched by the paucity of facts about their production, it appears that ready-made clothes for children existed long before they were being made for grown-ups, and also that they were good enough to be bought by the aristocracy. In the absorbing record of the family life of the 3rd Duke of Hamilton, *The Days of Duchess Anne*, brought to life by Rosalind E. Marshall from family papers of the seventeenth century, there is a detailed account of the clothes of the children of this couple, who moved in the best society of the time, the Duke being attached to the Court of Charles II. Dr Marshall is worth quoting fully, because she so aptly summarizes the stages of children's dress in her time, as well as providing probably the earliest evidence of ready-to-wear clothing.

'The Duchess's sons and daughters spent the first weeks of their lives wrapped in swaddling bands . . . then as they grew older, they progressed to "carrying" frocks and coats and "going" (i.e. walking) frocks and coats. The little boys were dressed in petticoats for their first years and when he was five the Duchess's eldest son was still having petticoats made for him, although he also had linen trews. To a certain extent the local tailor provided the children's clothing, but very often the Duchess sent to Edinburgh. Henry Harper, one of the merchants there, sold her kitchen utensils from time to time, but he also specialized in garments for children and it is particularly interesting to note that although ready-to-wear clothes for adults did not come into vogue until long afterwards, by the early 1660s Henry Harper was selling a variety of children's ready-made clothes. In 1661, for instance, he sent the Duchess a bill for 'a boy's rose colour coat for 3 and 4 year old, 17/6: a boy's lemon colour coat for 3 and 4 years old 16/-; one large boy's and 2 large girls' white caps 7/-; 3 boys' white laced caps 6/-", and in the years which followed he supplied a long series of lemon, rose, sky blue and white carrying coats and going coats for boys and girls alike, white worsted stockings, and on one occasion "a large carnation taffeta bonnet with a white feather" at eight and sixpence. This must surely be one of the earliest examples of "mail order shopping". . . . It was not long before the children had discarded their baby clothes and were wearing garments which were miniature versions of their parents' clothing. When he was eleven the Earl of Arran went to Edinburgh with the family, and his father's tailor made for him a complete outfit of cloak, coat, justicoat and breeches, while John Muirhead was soon making up gowns for the girls along with the Duchess's own.'

In past centuries and probably until Victorian times children's clothes in the upper and middle classes were normally made by their parents' tailors and dressmakers after their very early years. There are numerous references, some of them already quoted, to the small boy's 'breeching' being marked by his first suit made by his father's tailor, and household accounts show mothers' and daughters' fashions being made by the same dressmakers. Among less exalted people children's clothes were usually made at home, by the mother, servants or the long-established visiting 'little dressmaker'. Cutting down adult clothes or adapting them to youthful needs was frequent – as it was again during World War II.

That this method of contriving clothes for children was very general in the 1880s is indicated by Flora Thompson, whose *Lark Rise to Candleford* is a precious record of traditional English village life, captured at the point of its disappearance. Girls, she says, often wore clothes cut down from those handed on by wealthier kinsfolk or given by their employers to members of the family who were in domestic service. Thus 'the hamlet had a fashion of its own, a year or so behind outside standards and strictly limited as to style and colour'. For Sundays 'clean, white, starched clothes' were the small girl's invariable wear. The packman, or pedlar had largely disappeared from Candleford, identified as Buckingham, and the neighbouring villages on which the stories centre, because 'people had taken to buying their clothes at the shops in the market town, where fashions were newer and prices lower', but one remained, with 'dress lengths and shirt-lengths and remnants to make up for the children; aprons and pinafores, plain and fancy.'

Fine sewing was going out. 'Ready-made clothes were beginning to appear in the shops, but those such as working people were able to buy were coarse, ugly and of inferior quality' and people still made their own underwear for this reason if they were at all fastidious: 'Their taste ran to plenty of trimming; lace and insertion and feather-stitching on undergarments, flounces on frocks.'

It also seems that the demand for good quality ready-made children's clothes in Victorian times rose first among the better-off and spread downwards, in contrast to those of adults, which catered at first for the cheaper end of the fashion trade. The *Mother's Home Book*, one of the many treatises on domestic economy which were much in demand, says of children's ready-made clothes: 'The purchasing of these, happily, does not now apply itself only to persons in the possession of a good income, as it did formerly. A few years back only the rich dreamed of buying their children's, especially their boys', attire ready-made at an outfitter's, or of having them made up by a tailor. But now . . . unless a mother be a very good amateur tailoress indeed, her labour is somewhat lost as regards fit, style and fashion.'

The frilly, lavishly trimmed white dresses and pinafores of the late nineteenth and early twentieth century small girl were ideally suited to the ever-improving sewing machine and they feature in catalogues of leading stores. Dickins and Jones in 1895 devoted a considerable amount of space in a catalogue to young girls' attire, ranging from cashmere and muslin dresses and smocked dresses in vicuna, zephyr and silk to a great variety of sailor costumes, 'the most comfortable dress for children, suitable for all seasons' and offered in a great variety of materials. Other store catalogues also featured a wide variety of children's off-the-peg clothes, Libertys being particularly enterprising here.

Boys' suits from Victorian times also lent themselves easily to manufacturing processes, and advertisements for them appeared widely during the second half of last century. Ready-made clothes for boys and girls must have been made mainly by the overworked, underpaid home workers or in the crowded 'sweat shops', both of which were a blot on fashion in the nineteenth century and even later and which constituted much of the garment trade.

The dress of the middle-class child of the years immediately before World War I is described by Geraldine Symons in *Children in the Close*. There are still the 'white frocks and sashes' going down to the drawing room, but for most occasions clothes were made by a little dressmaker: 'When we were quite young, our clothes were sometimes made by Fanny Parsons . . . Fittings took place in the front parlour.' Underwear was, for winter, flannel drawers, woollen gaiters, stays, combinations, but in summer Liberty bodices, vests, cotton drawers, with, all the year round, petticoats – probably mainly bought at shops and stores. Incidentally, at the seaside these children all paddled with frocks and petticoats tucked into drawers.

In the first decades of this century and probably earlier another important source of clothes for children was a now vanished retail outlet – a drapery and haberdashery shop which also had a small workroom attached. Often a family business with a woman owner assisted by her daughters, such a shop was much sought after by middle-class mothers who took a pride in their

daughters' appearance and had their own views about style and materials, including the vogue for dressing sisters alike which prevailed in the first two decades of this century, until assertive girls rebelled against this assault upon their identity. Such shops with their personal appeal were the precursors of the later 'Madam' shops and of the more recent boutiques, which have spread from adult fashions to those of children. A few high class speciality children's shops flourished in the 1920s and 1930s.

The large-scale manufacture of children's clothes, like those of adults, made great strides in size and quality in the years after World War I, stimulated not only by the greater simplicity of all fashion but also by the notable improvements in technical processes developed during the mass production of service uniforms. Ready-to-wear became the general choice for the young of all classes. Except in rare cases the rise of branded names was a later development, both in adults' and children's wear. A few of the latter existed and still survive and flourish. 'Chilprufe for children' was almost an adage in every nursery from early in this century, a name revered for outerwear as well as underwear. Burberrys also had children's outerwear ready-made and to order.

Viyella, today regarded as having a special cachet for the young, ran true to historical form in that it started with adults in mind and extended its scope to include infants and children only when they offered a strong and expanding market. The yarn-spinning firm which became William Hollins and Co. in 1846 was established in 1784 but moved into weaving only in 1891 and registered the brand name Viyella (taken from its Via Gellia mills) in 1894 for men's shirts and nightshirts. It was the first cloth of its kind to be registered – and advertised – in this way. They began to make up their own ranges for men and women in 1903 and gradually moved into the children's area too. This was developed in the years between the wars, with great progress in the 1930s both in young fashions and in non-shrink properties. When the Utility scheme was introduced they added a new fabric Dayella in order to avoid lowering the quality of Viyella as regulations required. Dayella was so successful for babies' and children's clothing that the Board of Trade ruled that it should be reserved exclusively for that purpose. This spurred the company to make children's wear a major part of their clothing operation in the post-war years and thereby to become fashion leaders in this area.

When branded names began to multiply, in the 1930s, they were in many cases short-lived. As in the women's fashion trade, the once-familiar children's

107 Well-dressed children of
1935–6: Chilprufe

wear names have mostly vanished. But by an odd chain of events Ladybird, now the biggest specialist manufacturers of children's fashions in Europe, entered the British market in the years between the wars. They did so by a process as long and complicated as the emergence of today's immense young market itself and to a degree representative of how that market evolved. They did not start in the fashion trade, but began in textiles in Central Europe, which, long afterwards, was to be the origin of many of the top names in the fashion trade. In 1688 the Psaold family first started as weavers in Fleisen, a small town in Bohemia. In 1768 Johannes Adam Pasold set up his first knitwear frame and by the early twentieth century the Pasolds were running a flourishing export business, mainly in women's fleecy knickers, 80 per cent of them for Britain. The 1929 financial crisis in Britain, plus import duties and the depression, wrought havoc with imports. So three young Pasold brothers, Eric, Rolf and Ingo, by then in charge of the firm, though the oldest of them was only 26 and the other two 18 and 16, made the big move to Langley, near Slough in South-East England.

They built a factory on a site where they still operate and, with some of their staff and their own special circular weft knitting machines, went on making fleecy knickers as before. With local labour and new equipment they expanded and when fleecy knickers went out of fashion they switched to ripple cloth dressing gowns, for adults and children, and also made vests for Woolworths to sell at 6d. each, the then top price for that famous pioneer multiple.

Diversification proceeded apace after World War II, when they had made service clothing, and the Ladybird trade mark and motif were acquired just after the war from Klingers of Edmonton. From then on the company concentrated entirely on children's wear. The first big break into this market came when, in 1948, they made the first children's T-shirts ever produced in England – and found them unsaleable, except for export to Canada, for nearly two years. Buyers in Britain said they looked like interlock vests and that the public would not give up coupons for them – as they still had to, for another year. When 30 dozen were, in desperation, supplied to Swan and Edgar on sale or return – against the firm's practice – and were advertised by that store, the tide suddenly turned. T-Shirts began to sell – at 4s. 11d. to start with – and became big business. 'For years', said the agent responsible for launching them, 'we were quite unable to cope with the exceptional demand.'

Ladybird has continued to grow ever since. T-shirts have become a feature of almost every wardrobe, infinite in their variety, the pride of every child and equally in favour with adults. Ladybird are still to the fore in new T-shirt styles for the young, specializing in multi-coloured designs covering the whole surface of the tubular knitted fabric which was the Company's particular innovation in those first T-shirts for children. In the first boom output was 36,000 T-shirts a day, and the fashion bonanza shows no signs of abating.

In early days the Ladybird range was limited, as was usual in the children's market. Items would stay in it for years, the seasons being marked by a few additions and deletions and not by a complete changeover. But through the 1950s children's fashions were becoming a vast and growing market and variety was constantly being sought. Ladybird introduced flame-resistant nightwear and flame-resistant nylon in 1961 and in 1964 brought in their first co-ordinates: 'Autumn will be the first Ladybird Mix and Match season', they announced. In 1968 Rolf Pasold in his chairman's report, summed up the recent history of children's fashions aptly when he said: 'The past ten years have seen a revolution in children's wear. While quality, value and fit remain as important as ever, the emphasis is on style. New materials and production facilities on the one hand and higher living conditions on the other, have provided designers with undreamed of opportunities. In their exuberance they have run riot and turned children's wear into a fashion industry so fast that less flexible makers fell by the wayside. It was not easy for us, the largest mass producers of children's clothes, to make the conversion.... We have ... geared outselves to produce fashion garments on a mass production basis, a task which a few years ago seemed almost impossible.'

In that year they had a turnover of £16,000,000, a profit of £2,000,000 before taxation and exports of over £1,500,000. Figures for recent years are not available, because the company has been a member of the Coats-Paton Group from 1968.

From the start Ladybird have themselves carried out every stage of manufacture. At Langley they have their own knitting mill, dye and print works, n.aking-up plant and distributing organization, all under one roof. Yarns of all types go in at one end and the completed range of some 2500 items for children up to 14 years of age comes out at the other. Ladybird today still has a family connection, with Udo Geipel, a cousin of the Pasold brothers, as Chairman, since the retirement of the Pasolds.

Since 1962 Chilprufe has been a subsidiary of Ladybird, but before then, through the years, this company had updated its image, dropping adult outerwear and such items as children's quilted binders, body belts, stay bands, combinations, head flannels and directoire knickers, all of which feature in old catalogues, some of them up to the 1930s. They were succeeded by buster

108 Chilprufe dressed youngsters like this in 1952

suits and jumper suits and later they added track suits, briefs, tights, trews and trousers in the 1950s. BabyChic is also made by the same group.

Today there are Ladybird factories at Glasgow, Stranraer, Coatbridge, Plymouth, Crediton, Belfast and Leicester, another in Portugal and a company in Canada making a special range for that market. They have 2500 employees in the U.K., more than 3000 altogether. They use their name everywhere except in the U.S.A. and Spain, but in France it is also registered as Cochinelle and in Germany as Marienkaefer. The motif is universal. They export about 15 percent of their output to around 100 countries and change their range twice a year.

They are the spearhead of the now accepted principle that children's clothes are designed to please children and not to please parents – though today's parents are also pleased by the arrangement. That the children are their target is indicated by the style of the vast advertising and promotion schemes run by Ladybird in recent years, many of them involving tie-ups with stores and shops. Advertisements are directed at children and competitions are run for children. There are treasure hunts, Ladybird story books about the adventures of a family of actual ladybirds. Editorial type advertisements have been run in children's periodicals, including a Libby Ladybird page, with pictures about travel and the right clothes for the well-dressed child at home and abroad. There is even a Ladybird Adventure Club, promoted by strip cartoons in children's annuals.

More and more variety and quicker change is the keynote of today's production, says their chief designer, Malcolm Thompson. The teenager has been supplanted by the subteenager as the spearhead of young fashion and the arbiter of taste, he declares. In the last few years leadership has passed to the eight to ten year olds. Children have a big say in what they wear from the age of about five, and parents accept this. It is difficult to get the public to

109   Part of today's variety, demanded by the young market. From the Ladybird range

realize that the cost of making-up children's clothes is almost as big as for adults, but people will pay for what is new and enterprising, and that is what children demand.

Children go for everything that has been denied them in the past, says Mr Thompson. They are hooked on strong, bright colours instead of the timid pastels parents used to choose. They want something different all the time. They reject conventional party clothes after the age of about four, and for special occasions will turn up in super-jeans and super-T-shirts, but never in orthodox suits or dresses. Little girls stop wanting long Kate Greenaway dresses after about six years old, when they join the jeans brigade, and they are very conscious that there are jeans *and* jeans. Boys think likewise; at the age of six or seven they are as emphatic as a Regency Buck about the cut of a trouser leg, the angle of a hip pocket.

Marks and Spencer's biggest strides into the children's market in their 252 stores in the U.K. have, surprisingly, been made very recently. Until 1975 their children's department was attached to the adult one, but from then there has been a separate children's wear group, with sections for boys and girls and further sub-divisions into knitwear, dresses, coats and underwear. These have been extended continuously, with the ranges from early 1976 including ages from nine to 14 instead of, as previously, stopping at ten or 11. In design they work closely with their manufacturers in a planned system of co-operation with their own designers. A classic school range is a recent development. Notable at present is their success in the European market for children, especially with tartan capes, skirts, blouses and dresses, some of them in trendy styles, and with denims, including pinafores and culottes. Other successful lines are duffle coats and dungarees for children of all ages. These are proving successful in both Paris and Brussels. They also do good business in children's wear in Canada. About 40 stores in Canada trade as Marks and Spencer, the rest of the 150 total trade under other names.

In general, hard-wearing clothes for children are best-sellers, but fashion is becoming increasingly important – and fashion today means rapid and frequent changes and variations, mainly within the area of casuals.

How the mass market for infants' and children's wear has developed in recent years is effectively illustrated by British Home Stores, When the group started in 1928, with a maximum price of 1s. for its goods, no drapery departments existed. In 1929 they raised their top price to five shillings and started to sell some textiles, including children's and infants' wear. The price limit disappeared during World War II and since then a policy of upgrading their merchandise in style and quality has been pursued with increasing energy and growing attention to exclusive lines. Early on in this process they had an infants' line called *Twinkle*, but in 1960 *Prova* became the company's sole brand name. From that time their infants' and children's wear departments have progressively been enlarged.

In a broad survey of this section they say that recent years have seen some outstanding changes, reflecting new attitudes to children among customers at their 100 branches all over the country. To start with they used to run similar ranges for an age group extending from 2–13 years, but now it is highly important to identify their market much more closely and they find well-

110 What they want to wear. Plaid dungarees from British Home Stores, 1976

111   Denim is much in demand;
Matchmaker battle jacket and
jeans by British Home Stores,
worn with T-shirts

defined differences between the needs of the 1–2, 3–5, 5–8 and 9 onwards age groups. These needs are constantly under survey by their team of some eight children's wear buyers, who work closely with their manufacturers to keep pace with the increasingly rapid movements of fashion. Buyers also travel abroad including Europe and America, to study trends in what has become an international area of fashion.

The idea of one range a year, which once prevailed, has gone by the board, and the life-style of an individual line is becoming shorter and shorter, ranging from weeks to at most six months. In general they find that adults set the fashions and children follow on. This is seen at its strongest in the greatly increased demand for casuals, separates and co-ordinates from the time when children start having definite ideas of their own about what they want to wear. Today this is about six years old and even less. The denim look, product of the teenage move towards casual dress and to the fore when money is again tight, is as dominant in the young market as among adults. Girls' outerwear, a notably expanding market, featured co-ordinated dresses, jackets, trousers, waistcoats, skirts and pinafores as a leading line for autumn 1976.

School uniforms have relaxed so much in requirements that they have moved to a large degree out of the specialist departments to multiple stores, and B.H.S. are today well equipped to meet the main needs – grey shorts and pullovers, navy blazers, skirts and pinafores, duffle coats and raincoats, white shirts and blouses. Uniforms, once eclectic, have come to terms with everyday wear. That means emphasis on value for money, vigilance over production standards and a sound assessment of whether a garment is needed to last for one year or five.

Sizing, always a special problem in the children's market, has been re-structured recently by British Home Stores, who now rely on measurements and not ages and give special attention to height. They constantly try out their merchandize on a wide variety of children before it goes to stores, checking not only on sizes and fittings but also on styling, colours and materials. In this project it is noted that the 9–14 age group is newly emerging as a very important and articulate part of the market, with emphatic views on what it wants to wear and vigorous rejection of what does not match up to its needs and wishes.

112 Duffle coats have become school uniform

14 *Present Day*

Infants being, of all human kind, the least able to communicate their views except by yells which even modern psychology probably frequently misinterprets, were among the last to be delivered from the trammels of time-honoured clothing. Even the most enlightened mothers continued to be daunted by the difficulties and cost involved in trying to put young babies into rational, functional, manageable clothing. It was, like elder children's clothing, largely a production problem which could be met only by its recognition as a special area of manufacture and not, as in the past, a mere appendage of the clothing industry – or even of the children's sector of that industry.

One big new recognition of the infant's needs came when, in the 1950s, his liberation from the long dresses of centuries began. The instigator of this major break-through from tradition was Walter Artzt, an inventive business man who had gone to New York from Vienna as a young man and had been responsible for a number of innovations in textile machinery and in fabrics. It was as an observant grandfather that he introduced in America a one-piece coverall suit for babies, made from a new stretch fabric which he invented for this purpose and patented, as he did with his design. The suit was the acme of comfort and ease, with feet, cuffs which could become mitts, and poppers between the legs. It has progressively been improved and is now internationally known and marketed as Babygro.

The British company, wholly U.K. in structure, but with Walter Artzt, still resident in New York, as its chairman, was established in 1962 in a converted schoolhouse in Scotland with 20 employees. This is now the 'think tank' for every new invention and marketing development in the brand as a whole, all over the world. With four factories in Kirkcaldy, Cowdenbeath and Arbroath and over 800 employees, Babygro also has head offices in the West End of London and is the largest supplier of stretchwear for babies to stores and shops in the UK.

Following the new fashion emphasis given to even the youngest child's attire in recent years, Babygro now introduce a new range twice a year. From the basic stretch coverall made for all ages from birth to two years they have extended their range to include rompers, crawlers, T-shirts, underwear, tights and socks. They now use fashionably strong colours, appliquéd animal and other motifs, and are alert innovators in design as well as leaders in technical know-how, featuring no-seam shoulders and armholes and a patented 'grotoe' in recent Babygro garments and continually improving upon their fabrics. Their range is sold everywhere and their brand name has become almost part of the English language – but is still exclusively theirs.

A crucial advance in re-thinking the design, manufacture and selling of infants' clothing in Britain was taken when, in 1961, Selim K. Zilkha took the first steps that led to the establishment of Mothercare, the only chain group to concentrate wholly on expectant mothers and the young from birth until five years – until the spring of 1976, when it extended the range to ten-year-olds. In addition to clothing, every need of the child is its concern, from feeding bottles to furniture and toiletries to toys.

Selim Zilkha's immediate impetus to make his way into what was then estimated to be a £100,000,000 a year market came from his conviction that there was a 'market gap' in infants' and young children's clothes and equipment, which could and should be filled. He had no links with the clothing trade, but his background lay to some extent within the familiar geographical pattern of fashion trade personalities. He is a member of a Middle East family, though in his case a banking one. He was educated mainly in the U.S.A., graduated from an American college and is an American citizen.

Mothercare, which he started with a clothing man, Barney Goodman, and of which he has been chairman and managing director from the outset, got off the ground with a know-how agreement with the already successful French Prenatal group, which lasted till 1965. It also followed in many ways the pattern for general merchandizing set by the supremos of the business,

113 The original stretch coverall, the Babygro, which was a major break-through for infants' wear in the 1950s, first in America, then in Britain and all over Europe

114 Today's full range from Babygro includes this crawler with helicopter motif and matching T-shirt, in sizes up to 2 years

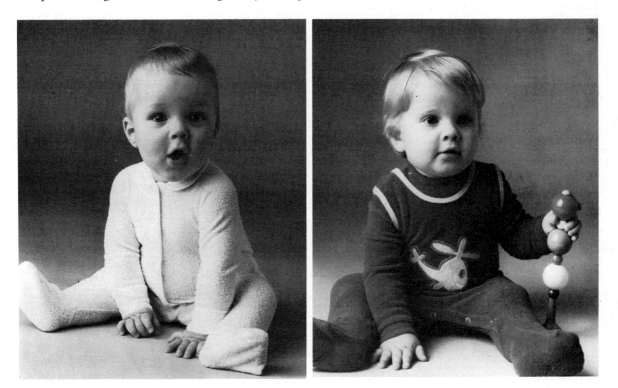

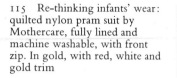

115 Re-thinking infants' wear: quilted nylon pram suit by Mothercare, fully lined and machine washable, with front zip. In gold, with red, white and gold trim

Marks and Spencer. The first trading year was 1963, the first one to show a profit was 1965. Between 1966 and 1976 the number of stores rose continuously from 60 to 174, sales from £2,762,000 to £59,044,195, employees from 590 to nearly 4,000, catalogue distribution from 605,000 to 5,902,000. The 1976 trading profit was £8,524,348; profit after tax was £4,054,600. The company went public in 1972, when it proved unexpectedly the year's largest share issue. Exports in 1976 were a record £5,362,000, nearly £2,900,000 of them to the group companies overseas.

Most recently of all, Mothercare made history in the British children's wear trade when, in July 1976, it acquired the Dekon Corporation, which operates 114 retail outlets in 27 states in the U.S.A., selling maternity clothing. Surprisingly, no specialist maternity and babywear shops had previously existed in America. This reversal of the traditional U.S. leadership in children's fashions gave Mothercare a major foothold in the American market, with a potential far greater than that of its British operation. It was a complete Anglo-American alliance, with Selim Zilkha adding the chairmanship of the U.S. company to that of the parent British one, and three British executives moving to America. The plan was to introduce the full Mothercare range into the Dekon shops, the company being renamed Mothercare with this purpose in view.

The rise of Mothercare has coincided with and has also been to a large extent instrumental in producing the biggest-ever change in the dressing of the infant and young child. The company's director of merchandizing and the only woman on the board, Marlene David, says: 'Nothing has happened to our organization that hasn't happened in the world outside. Life now is more free and easy. Children's clothes have changed radically.' Their catalogues reflect the change – the early ones show clothes that now appear fussy and formal in comparison with today's functional, easy-care ones.

The biggest change of all is probably in the dress of the infant. The long dress, if worn at all, is now limited to the first two or three months and the christening ceremony – but even here it probably is of nylon and in 1970 a romper was a suggested alternative for a boy. The almost universal attire is the stretch body-suit, which Mothercare call Babystretch, a kind of outer casing, complete with feet and mitts for cold weather, fastened with poppers between the legs and made of one of the new man-made stretch materials that have revolutionized baby-wear. There is also an all-encasing sleeping bag. In both of these the child, as in the days of swaddling, is back in a cocoon – but

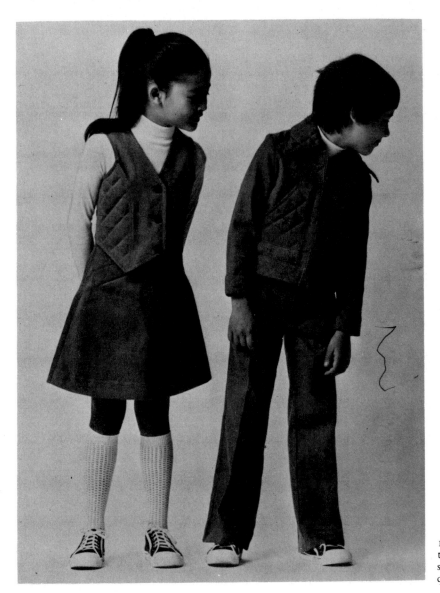

116 Free-and-easy clothes for today by Mothercare. Blue suèded denim co-ordinates, quilted for warmth

today's cocoon has complete freedom of movement. The space-age child's first outfit is a kind of space suit.

There are still some dresses for party wear for boy and girl babies, but they are mostly short smocks with matching pants. The first denim suit from Mothercare is now made to fit a child of three months. From then, denim is as much part of the nursery as of the schoolroom, with ranges of trousers, suits and dresses in sizes starting from the nine-months-old wearer. Stretch denim came into the range in 1972, which was also the year of the cat-suit for the young. Small girls went into colourful tights in the mid-sixties, when women took to tights. Bright colours, playsuits, track suits, now come in the smallest sizes. Little girls have almost ceased to wear petticoats, but have taken to occasional long party dresses, like their mothers and like the little girls of 200 years ago and of the Kate Greenaway era a century later, as if to show that in fashion there is nothing new under the sun. Small boys are perhaps likewise going back to the skeleton suit, for most of them have settled firmly for long trousers, with shorts only in the hottest weather.

It has been said that the directors of Mothercare can frequently be seen at the huge windows of their Watford factory with binoculars directed to the primary school playground below. They are studying what children actually wear, consulting their customers who, they would probably say, are always right, however young they may be. That is the crucial, the hitherto undreamt-of thing.

As in adult fashions, the rise of large-scale production of young people's clothes has run parallel to the proliferation of highly individualistic, usually trendy outlets, often specializing in one particular age-group or style. Children's boutiques here also opened in hundreds and in infinite variety.

The child's freedom of choice in dress today extends to every area, even to some degree showing itself in school uniform, normally dictated by the school head. This has even happened at Eton itself, where the first signs of the boys having an increasing say in what they wore were apparent some considerable time ago. In *Changing Eton*, published in 1937, L.S.R. Byrne and E.L. Churchill point out that dress in recent times has been 'only one of the unwritten regulations made by the boys themselves.' In the past 30 to 40 years, for instance, the cloth used for trousers had varied greatly, by the boys' choice. A group photograph of 1903 shows various tweeds and other materials worn by the boys of one house, but suddenly, about 1905, stripes, similar to today's, appeared, and, by the boys' decree, became universal. Between 1880 and 1890, the same authors say, boys had already decided for themselves when to go into stick-up collars. In 1911 soft shirts were adopted, and soon afterwards shoes replaced boots.

Mr Patrick Strong, Keeper of Eton College Library and Collections today and an old Etonian, recalls that in his schooldays and up to the 1950s or early 1960s boys under 5ft 4in tall continued to wear the Eton jacket. When he took up his present post in 1966 only choristers still wore Eton jackets and Eton collars, but they soon discarded them. Now tails and striped trousers are worn by all. The 24 members of the select Eton society, Pop, founded in 1820, still retain their privilege of wearing sponge-bag trousers, fancy waist-

117 Colourful gear for 1976: patchwork trousers and plaid top by Viyella

118 Frilly dress in contrasting materials, by Viyella

119   Ponchos from America in
plaid and striped wool, a fashion
story of the 1970s among young
and old

120   Small boys in grey flannel
suits flock back to Cheam to
meet the new pupil, the Prince
of Wales, in 1957

coats and braid round their tail coats. By an unwritten law the bottom waist-coat button is left unfastened.

Today, says Mr Strong, there are all sorts of 'boy quirks' about the school uniform. Rules that have nothing to do with the authorities are rigidly followed. Thus no mackintoshes may be worn. The overcoat collar must not be turned up except by members of 'Pop', who also have a similar un-written right to roll their umbrellas, which no other boys may do. General clothes rules have been relaxed substantially. For winter games and after classroom hours tweed jackets are allowed. In summer term boys can change out of uniform for afternoon school and even for chapel and can wear what they choose, so long as the result is neat and tidy. It is up to housemasters to decide whether such revolutionary breaks with tradition as jeans and fancy shirts are admissible.

Outside Eton college buildings and grounds, however, recognizable uniforms are compulsory. The last word over uniforms rests with the Provost and Fellows of the college. Today's headmaster personally would like the suits updated, but so far by the concensus of official opinion the traditional tails remain. The uniform, it is pointed out, is practical; boys outgrow tails more slowly than ordinary jackets. About a third of all Eton's uniforms come from Tom Brown's High Street shop, established in the 1700s on its present site as tailors and woollen drapers. They recall that in 1875 the complete Eton uniform cost £4 10s. In 1949 the coat cost nine guineas and a complete suit 18 guineas, plus purchase tax. In 1965 the suit cost £25 and in 1975, £45. Cutting is done in stock sizes by the shop, but the making-up goes to large-scale manufacturers. Another blow to tradition is that stick-up collars can be of paper, disposable in the modern manner.

In general school uniforms have shown a relaxation and a closer alignment with fashion in recent years. For boys the once proudly worn school cap has all but disappeared; it would be unwearable with the long hair of many of today's schoolboys, approved even by many public schools, and in any case would be an anachronism in the male wardrobe.

Surprisingly, some girls' schools, mainly exclusive boarding ones, have succumbed to the nostalgic note of some women's fashions and have reverted to the straw boater generally discarded nearly half a century ago. Incidentally, it now costs £4.75 in one leading London store's school uniforms department, instead of about 2s. 11d. in the 1920s. For extra chic it comes in navy blue and green and even has old-fashioned elastic to keep it on. Some of the more exclusive girls' schools have also gone back to the long capes introduced at St Leonards last century. In green, blue, red and other colours, often with contrasting bright linings and with hoods, they crowd the rails at Peter

121 Casual uniforms at Gordonstoun, the Prince of Wales's next school

122   School history was made
in 1970 when the first 24 girls
were admitted to the long-
established boys-only King's
School, Ely. In uniform capes
they were welcomed by the
more informally clad boys

Jones's in Sloane Square and other specialist school uniform departments.
More practical than school coats, as well as more interesting.

Trends today for girls in uniform are moving towards short, pleated skirts
rather than shorts for games. Skirts and blouses or modern-style pinafore
dresses are also favoured, and the old-time gym tunic is right out. Blazers
come in a rainbow array of colours. The occasional acceptance of trousers as
school uniform for girls is the main very recent innovation; otherwise changes
are not frequent, though cotton dresses for summer keep fairly close to
general fashions and are usually pretty, smart and made in a choice of colours.

A rather unexpected sidelight on girls' school uniforms is the fact that many
schools drop uniforms completely for the sixth form, members of which are
allowed to wear whatever they like, even jeans. The North London Collegiate
School, which has adopted this practice, and which also allows trousers as
school uniform, says that up to their later teens girls like uniform and that it
promotes confidence and a feeling of solidarity. Then it becomes repressive,
is disliked and resented. Problems of frustration are ironed out by its abolition
and, surprisingly, discipline and morale improve.

Boys' school uniforms have remained more conservative, with grey flannel
suits still widely worn, and flannels and blazers the general rule from expensive
boarding schools to the comprehensives. Unlike girls, boys do not want to
abandon it at the sixth form stage. There is a curious parallel here in the fact

that the businessman still wears what is more or less a uniform – the lounge
suit – but the businesswoman, in face of the equality claimed by the 1976 Sex
Discrimination Act, shows no such tendency, but dresses in her own individual
way. It is a curious psychological phenomenon, though not relevant here.

Relevant, however, to the present state and future development of children's
fashions is the strange phenomenon of jeans and denims and the spread of them
from the young to nearly all ages in all countries, at least in the western world.
Sales go up and up. At the 1976 Cologne Fashion Fair devoted to children's
wear it was noted that in the previous year 17.1 million pairs of jeans had
been sold in West Germany, a leader in young fashions, to children under
15 years of age. Children's denim suits accounted for 70 per cent of their
clothes market, while 30 per cent of all girls' skirts were made of denim, all
these being increases on the previous year's sales.

Denim, in the words of a writer on children's fashions commenting on
this phenomenon, is now 'more than a fashion. . . . It's practically become an
extension of our skin. I can't remember anything else sweeping the whole
world in the way denim has in the past decade, so there must be a reason for
it. And of course the reason is obvious, it's practical and hard-wearing,
especially for children, looks good in most cases and is easy and comfortable
to wear. It's a great leveller in the way usually claimed for school uniforms. . . .
It's fine for unisex clothes, which aren't a bad thing for young children.'

123 and 124 Variety in today's
fashions: left to right,
workmanlike dungarees, long
dresses for parties, by Ladybird

These are probably the main reasons. They put the ball firmly in the children's court so far as this area of clothes leadership is concerned. Children want comfort and freedom in what they wear and in the century of the child they have brought it not only to their own clothes but also, for the first time, to all fashion. Two hundred years ago the first steps towards comfort and freedom were taken, when educationalists, reformers and poets recognized that children were not just imperfect adults who should be forced into adulthood as quickly as possible but distinct entities with their own needs. The small boy's skeleton suit and the small girl's simple muslin dress were the first comfortable fashions for centuries and their influence soon spread through fashion for all.

After the lapse into discomfort and pretentiousness in Victorian times children have again led the way to comfort and ease in dress in a century in which they are accorded immense attention. Their denims and duffle coats, bright shirts and sweaters, T-shirts and anoraks are as much part of the adult wardrobe as of their own smaller one. Children and grown-ups are again dressing alike, but in a new way. It is a way that breaks all the established rules of fashion. The styles do not start at the top, among the wealthy and leisured who have traditionally been the leaders of fashion. There is no conventional status symbol significance in them. They do not therefore go out of fashion on the grounds that they are not exclusive. The more general their adoption the better.

The social upheaval of our times is nowhere recorded so explicitly as in the clothes we wear. These clothes make a nonsense of the complicated fashion story of the past. Jean Muir, a top name in today's world of clothes, sums up the contemporary attitude as 'people simply want nice clothes to wear.' And they want to decide for themselves what that means, not to follow the leadership of Paris or anywhere else. It is exactly what the child regards as the sensible attitude to clothes. It could not be bettered. It is doubtful if it ever will be in the kind of world we live in today – or tomorrow.

Bibliography

Aglaia, *John Heddon*, 1893–4

Ballin, Ada, *The Science of Dress*, Sampson Low, 1885
Binder, Pearl, *Muffs and Morals*, Harrap, 1953
Binder, Pearl, *The Peacock's Tail*, Harrap, 1958
Borer, Mary Cathcart, *Willingly to School*, Lutterworth, 1976
Bradby, H.C., *Rugby*, George Bell, 1900
Brooke, Iris, *English Children's Costume since 1775*, A. & C. Black, 1930
Brooke, Iris, *English Costume 1900–1950*, Methuen, 1951
Buck, Anne, *Victorian Costume and Costume Accessories*, H. Jenkins, 1961
Burkstall, Sara A., *Retrospect & Prospect*, Longman Green, 1933
Byrne, L.S.R. & Churchill, E.L., *Changing Eton*, Cape, 1937

Caplin, Roxey A., *Health and Beauty*, Kent, 1864 (3rd Edition)
Clare, Rev. William, *The Historic Dress of the English Schoolboy*, Society for the Preservation of Ancient Customs, London, 1939
Clark, Kenneth, *Another Part of the Wood*, G. Allen and Unwin, 1974
Cohn, Nik, *Today there are No Gentlemen*, Weidenfeld & Nicholson, 1971
Cook, Hartley Kemball, *Those Happy Days*, G. Allen and Unwin, 1945
Costume Society Journal No. 8, 1974, Alan Mansfield on 'Dress of the English Schoolchild'
Cunnington, C.W. & Phillis, *Handbook of English Costume in the Eighteenth Century*, Faber, 1957
Cunnington, Phillis and Buck, Anne, *Children's Costume in England 1300–1900*, A. & C. Black, 1965
Cunnington P. and Lucas C., *Occupational Costume in England from the 11th century to 1914*, A. & C. Black, 1967
Cunnington, P. and Mansfield, A., *English Costume for Sport and Outdoor Recreation*, A. & C. Black, 1969

Day, Thomas, *The History of Sandford and Merton*, 3 parts: 1783–1787–1789, corrected and revised by Cecil Hartley, Routledge
Douglas, Mrs, *The Gentlewoman's Book of Dress*, Henry & Co, 1895
Du Maurier, Daphne, *The Young George Du Maurier*, Peter Davies, 1951

Earle, Alice Morse, *Child Life in Colonial Days*, Macmillan, 1899
Evans, Mary, *Costume Throughout the Ages*, Lippincott, 1950

Fielding, Sarah, *The Governess or Little Female Academy*, A facsimile representation of the first edition of 1749, OUP, 1968
Fletcher, Ronald, *The Parkers at Saltram 1769–1789*, B.B.C., 1970

Gardiner, D., *English Girlhood at School,* O.U.P., 1929
Garland, Madge, *Fashion*, Penguin Books, 1962
Gerson, Noel B., *George Sand*, R. Hale, 1973
Godfrey E., *English Children in the Olden Times*, Methuen, 1907
Grant, Elizabeth, *Memoirs of a Highland Lady*, ed. Angus Davidson, Murray, 1950

Haldane, Elizabeth, *From One Century to Another*, A. MacLehose, 1937
Haldane, Louisa Kathleen, *Friends and Kindred*, Faber, 1961
Haldane, Mary Elizabeth, *Record of a Hundred Years*, Hodder & Stoughton, 1925
Hartnell, Norman, *Royal Courts of Fashion*, Cassell, 1971
Haweis M., *The Art of Dress*, Chatto & Windus, 1879
Howe, Bea, *Arbiter of Elegance*, Harvill Press, 1967
Hughes, Thomas, *Tom Brown's Schooldays*, Macmillan, 1857

Ironside, Janey, *Janey*, M. Joseph, 1973

Jackson M., *What they Wore*, Allen & Unwin, 1936
Junior Age, 1936–76.

Kamm, Josephine, *Hope deferred: Girls' Education in English History*, Methuen, 1965
Kamm, Josephine, *How different from Us*, Bodley Head, 1958
King-Hall, Magdalen, *The Story of the Nursery*, R. & K. Paul, 1958

Lamb, Felicia & Pickthorn, Helen, *Locked-up Daughters*, Hodder & Stoughton, 1968
Laver, James, *Children's Fashions in the 19th Century*, Batsford, 1953
Laver, James, *Taste and Fashion*, Harrap, 1937, revised 1945
Lemprière, William, *A History of the Girls School of Christ's Hospital*, Cambridge U.P., 1924
Leslie, Shane, *The Oppidan*, Chatto & Windus, 1922
Lochhead M., *Their First Ten Years*, Murray, 1956
Longmate, Norman, *How we Lived Then*, Hutchinson, 1971
Lumsden, Louisa Innes, *Yellow Leaves*, Blackwood, 1932
Lyte, H.C. Maxwell, *A History of Eton College*, Macmillan, 1875

Mackenzie, Compton, *My Life and Times*, Octaves 1 and 2, Chatto & Windus, 1963–4
McClellan, Elizabeth, *History of American Costume*, Tudor Publishing Co.

N.Y., 1903

Mansfield A. and Cunnington P., *Handbook of English Costume in the 20th Century*, 1900–1950, Faber, 1973

Marshall, Rosalind E., *The Days of Duchess Anne*, Collins, 1973

Mathers, Helen, *Comin' Through the Rye*, H. Jenkins, 1875

Maxwell, Stuart and Hutchinson, Robin, *Scottish Costume 1150–1850*, A. & C. Black, 1958

Merrifield, Mrs, *Dress as a Fine Art*, Arthur Hall Virtue & Co., 1854

Mitford, Miss, *Our Village*, Harrap 1947, (reprint), original 1824–1832

Moore, D. Langley, *E. Nesbit*, Revised edn. E. Benn, 1967

Moore, D. Langley, *The Child in Fashion*, Batsford, 1953

Newton, Stella Mary, *Health, Art and Reason*, Murray, 1974

North, H. Roger, *The Lives of the Norths*, Ed. Augustus Jessopp, D.D., George Bell, 1890 (First published 1740–42, collected edition 1806)

Oakley, Ann, *Housewife*, Allen Lane, 1974

Opie, Iona and Peter, *The Classic Fairy Tales*, O.U.P., 1974

Panter-Downes, Mollie, *London War Notes*, Longman, 1972

Panton, J.E., *From Kitchen to Garret 1888*

Peck, Winifred, *A Little Learning*, Faber & Faber, 1952

Pinchbeck, Ivy and Hewitt, Margaret, *Children in English Society*, Routledge & Kegan Paul, 1969

Powell, Rosamond Bayne, *The English Child in the Eighteenth Century*, J. Murray, 1939

Raikes, Elizabeth, *Dorothea Beale of Cheltenham*, Constable, 1908

Ridley, Annie E., *Frances Mary Buss*, Longman Green, 1895

Ridley, Viscountess (ed.), *The Life and Letters of Cecilia Ridley*, Hart-Davis, 1958

Roe, F. Gordon, *The Georgian Child*, Phoenix House, 1961

Roe, F. Gordon, *The Victorian Child*, Phoenix House, 1959

St Leonards School 1877–1927, OUP, 1927

Settle, Alison, *English Fashion*, Collins, 1948

Sibbald S., *Memories of Susan Sibbald (1783–1812)*, edited Francis Paget Hett, Bodley Head, 1926

Sillar, Eleanor, *Edinburgh's Child*, Oliver & Boyd, 1961

Sitwell, Osbert, *Left Hand Right Hand*, Vol. 1, Macmillan, 1945

Smith, J.T., *Book for a Rainy Day*, Methuen (1845), new edition 1905

Steadman, F. Cicely, *In the Days of Miss Beale*, E.J. Burrow, 1931

Stoney, Barbara, *Enid Blyton*, Hodder & Stoughton, 1974

Strutt, Joseph, *A Complete View of the Dress and Habits of the People of England*, H.C. Bohn, 1842

Strutt, Joseph, *History of Costume*, Tabard Press, 1970 (reprint)

Stuart, Dorothy Margaret, *The Boy through the Ages*, Harrap, 1926

Stuart, Dorothy Margaret, *The Girl Through the Ages*, Harrap, 1933
Symons, Geraldine, *Children in the Close*, Batsford, 1959

Thompson, Flora, *Lark Rise to Candleford*, OUP, 1945 (as trilogy)
Thwaite, Ann, *Waiting for the Party*, Secker & Warburg, 1974
Townshend, Dorothea, *The Life and Letters of Endymion Porter*, T. Fisher
    Unwin, 1897

Uttley, Alison, *Ambush of Young Days*, Faber, 1937

Waller, Jane (ed), *Some Things for the Children*, Duckworth, 1974
Waugh, Nora, *Corsets and Crinolines*, Batsford, 1954
Webster, Thomas, assisted by the late Mrs Parkes, *Encyclopaedia of Domestic
    Economy*, Longman Green, 1844
Wilcox R. Turner, *Five Centuries of American Costume*, A. & C. Black, 1963
Wilcox R. Turner, *The Mode in Costume*, Scribner's, 1942
Wilcox R. Turner, *The Mode in Fashion*, Scribner's, 1948
Windeler, Robert, *Shirley Temple*, W.H. Allen, 1976
Wright, Thomas, *A History of Domestic Manners and Sentiments in England
    during the Middle Ages*, Chapman and Hall, 1862

Yarwood, Doreen, *English Costume*, Batsford 1952 (3rd Edn. 1973)
Yarwood, Doreen, *European Costume*, Batsford, 1975
Yass, Marion, *The Home Front, England 1939–1945*, Wayland, 1971
Yonge, Charlotte, *Village Children*, Gollancz Revivals, 1967

Index

References to illustrations are shown in *italics* by page numbers.